and

Predestination

Samuel Fisk

November, 1997

Penfold Book & Bible House
BICESTER, ENGLAND

First edition, September 1973
First paperback edition, June 1981
First British edition, 1997

Originally published in the USA by Loizeaux Brothers, Inc., Neptune, New Jersey, under the title *Divine Sovereignty and Human Freedom*
Published in the UK by Penfold Book & Bible House, Bicester, Oxfordshire, under the title *Election and Predestination*

ISBN: 1 900742 03 9

Other books by the Author:

Calvinistic Paths Retraced
Divine Healing Under The Searchlight
How To Deal With Mormonism
Confronting Jehovah's Witnesses
Speaking In Tongues In The Light Of Scripture
Letters To Teresa
40 Fascinating Conversion Stories
More Fascinating Conversion Stories

Printed by GTP, Glasgow, Scotland.

CONTENTS

FOREWORD

This is a timely book. First printed in the USA in 1973, some here already know it and speak of its value. One is delighted that it is again in print and now being published in the UK. This edition contains five extra appendices which further enhance the book. Clearly the author is thoroughly conversant with the subject and has spent much time in study and research to enable him to collate excerpts from so many expositors.

The Sovereignty of God is in no way undermined. How could God be God if He were not Sovereign? It should be remembered, however, that God has other attributes: Holiness; Righteousness; Love; Mercy; Grace; Longsuffering etc. These must all blend without one overshadowing another.

Augustine of Hippo (354-430) taught that God put a definite circle around the elect for the purpose of salvation. This was pursued by Calvin, taught by the Reformers and is still active and heavily publicized today. Of course there are many who do not accept Limited Atonement and the extremes of Calvinism, and are in full agreement that the gospel should be preached to the 'whosoever will' without exception, distinction, or reservation; but who nevertheless perceive that the standard and balanced view is that those who receive Christ were chosen by God to be saved.

There is, however, the more ancient view that election is corporate rather than individual, and that on conversion persons, foreknown by God, enter individually into the blessings which God has prepared, corporately, for those 'in Christ'. As a person entered the chosen nation Israel by birth, so today a person enters the chosen body, the church, by new birth. It is not that individuals are in the church because they are elect but that they are elect because they are in the church.

What then about Ephesians 1:4, "Chosen us in Him *before the foundation of the world*" and 2 Thessalonians 2:13 "God hath *from the beginning* chosen you to salvation"? Two different time notes, yet both used to support a 'before time selection process'. What do these verses then teach? What about Acts 13:48 'ordained'? Is foreknowledge to be understood as foreordination? These scriptures and questions, with many others, are all addressed and dealt with in a clear and helpful way in this book.

Whatever one's view of election and predestination, this book should not be ignored. It will richly repay not only reading, but also careful consideration, and should stimulate further study of the context of passages, as well as the meaning and usage of words. Good doctrine is important; it produces good practice.

Throughout this work the author is gracious and inoffensive in his manner. He is now aged but still alert in mind. The book has already been highly commended in the USA, and is known to be appreciated by many thoughtful students of the Word in the UK. This further recommendation seems so insignificant but my sincere desire is that the book, which is worthy of a wide circulation, will prove a blessing to many.

Samuel F. Johnston
Glasgow
Oct. 1997

PREFACE

It will be seen that the major portion of this work consists of quotations from others. We acknowledge our indebtedness to them. They have stated the case better than we could.

We cite such a wide range of authorities, not alone to display how many concur in the position herein set forth, or to demonstrate what prominent and well-known ones bore testimony in this direction, but for that which they say; that is, for the content of their expressions and for the reasons that they give for their views.

Albeit we have quoted many sources, this has by no means exhausted the available material. We have been impressed by the amount of pertinent data touching the subjects treated. Not only is material from further writers available, but more could also have been included from those quoted.

Most of the excerpts have been cut to the fewest possible words for simplicity, and to get right to the heart of the subject. To avoid involved issues and eliminate extraneous matter, we have included only what was regarded as pertinent, and therefore have indicated omissions where such omission was felt to be in the interest of conciseness, directness, and clarity.

In all excerpts emphasis is the original author's unless specifically designated as our own. In some of the more crucial cases we do repeat it, to stress that the emphasis is the original author's. Similarly, parentheses are in the original; brackets are ours unless stated as being in the original.

We have, of course, endeavored to represent fairly the

sentiment of the authors quoted. To be sure, some of these writers made other statements with a different emphasis, many of them holding to contrasting aspects of the truth. Here we aim chiefly to bring out that side of teaching which helps to an appreciation that there is this other side.

As a wide range of sources are elicited, those quoted may not always harmonize perfectly with one another, which is quite natural, as their points of departure are frequently different. But since it may prove interesting to see how various ones have expressed themselves on the general subject, we present material without trying to maintain complete unanimity of detail. The overall viewpoint, however, should be clear.

Some inconsistencies may seem to crop up where, after the limited meaning of a term is set forth, it is again seen reflecting the more popular meaning generally associated with it. For example, testimony is given to indicate that predestination and election have a meaning other than that commonly assumed, yet thereafter authors still use the words in a less carefully delineated manner. But this should not distract from the leading trend of thought under consideration.

Again, some writers suggest that these two lines of thought—divine sovereignty and human freedom—cannot be harmonized. Then others appear to be attempting just that, and this work itself may seem to be an effort in the same direction. However, this presentation is less an attempt to reconcile these two concepts than to show that, harmonized or not, both should be recognized, both should be included in any comprehensive view.

In gathering material for this treatise we avoided, on the whole, works of an Arminian nature, or those which might naturally be regarded as anti-Calvinistic.

In his student days the writer really wished that something just like this had been available to him. May it be helpful to some now in a similar position and to all others who may be interested.

SAMUEL FISK

CHAPTER 1

TWO CONCEPTS TO BE RECOGNIZED

God's revelation in Scripture is wonderful and full and complete. The more one studies it, the more one will be impressed with its breadth and range. It is sometimes difficult, with our limited understanding, to take in all that God has revealed in His Word. But we should always be ready to recognize the full-orbed truth, whether we can understand it or not, whether or not we can reconcile in our finite minds seemingly conflicting lines of teaching.

The more profound a truth is, the more difficult it is to comprehend its total sweep, as is the case in the matter of recognizing God's absolute sovereignty along with man's free and responsible will. But anything short of acknowledging both, it appears, would be to see only one side of the picture.

As we dip into the works of great Bible teachers we are impressed with their recognition of the two lines of truth here. Many have called to attention the need of seeing both elements. Let us observe some of these significant statements, and then see how other matters fit in.

Well-Known Men of God Express Themselves

On the two aspects of the truth, the following may be cited: Dr. Harry Ironside said, "Scripture plainly teaches election based upon God's foreknowledge. It is just as plain in its declarations of man's free will. All men are invited to accept the salvation that God has provided in Jesus Christ. 'Whosoever will' means just what it says." (*What's the Answer?* p. 54)

Dr. James M. Gray, of the Moody Bible Institute, said: "Take the lines indicated by the division into Calvinists and Arminians, for example. The apparently opposite positions for which these schools of religious thought stand are both found in the Bible, viz., God's sovereignty and man's free agency; but it would seem as though no one finite mind could hold both equally at the same time. How necessary, however, that both be duly emphasized!" (*Bible Problems Explained,* p. 45)

Dr. William L. Pettingill left this testimony: "The relation between God's sovereignty and elective purpose on the one hand and free grace and human responsibility on the other has perplexed the commentators throughout the ages. The best course is to believe all that God says and wait for Him to make it plain. God insists upon His sovereignty and also upon man's responsibility. Believe both and preach both, leaving the task of 'harmonizing' with Him." (*Bible Questions Answered,* p. 209)

Dr. C. I. Scofield said: "In all the Christian centuries men have endeavored to account, philosophically, for the apparent paradox of God's sovereign election and man's free will, but none have ever succeeded. Both are wholly true, but the connecting and reconciling truth has not been revealed." (*Scofield Bible Correspondence Course,* Vol. III, pp. 444-445)

Dr. R. A. Torrey began with the Congregationalists, but when we knew him he was with the Presbyterians, from which fact a strong emphasis on the divine side of things should be expected. Yet he said: "The Bible is the revelation of an infinite mind that presents all sides of the truth. . . . We are not to try to explain away the clear teaching of the Word of God as to the sovereignty of God on the one hand, nor the clear teaching of the Word of God as to the freedom of the human will on the other hand." (*The Importance and Value of Proper Bible Study,* pp. 80-81)

Another Presbyterian, and one who was also widely recognized, was Dr. Arthur T. Pierson, who not only demonstrated these truths, but showed the reasons for them: "Election, taught in the Word, must be consistent both with the sovereign will of God and the freedom of man; and if we cannot reconcile these two, it is because the subject is so infinitely lifted up above us. Man is free. There are in your heart and mine seven thunders that utter their voices, such as 'I am,' 'I think,' 'I reason,' 'I love,' 'I judge,' 'I choose,' 'I act.' And all these voices unite in affirming 'I am responsible.' Moreover, God Himself directly appeals to choice: He says, 'Why *will ye* die?' (Ezekiel 18:31) As the Apocalypse closes, we read, '*Whosoever will*, let him take the water of life freely.' Thus the last great invitation in God's Book is an appeal to the *will.* But—most startling of all—is Christ's lament over Jerusalem: 'How often *would I* have gathered thy children . . . even as a hen gathereth her chickens under her wings, and *ye would not.*' The yearning of God and the stubborn refusal of man are here put in clear antagonism. . . . Luke 15 contains one parable in three parts. The first represents the Shepherd seeking the lost sheep. . . . Thus far one might judge that all man has to do is passively to wait for God to come after him. But in the latter part of the parable we have the complementary truth, and from this part, if alone, it might be inferred that the sinner has everything to do, and God nothing; but putting the two together, we get the whole truth. . . . While Jesus never spoke of 'election' or 'predestination,' He gives us the parable of the sheepfold, of which He is the Door, and of the flock, of which He is the Shepherd; and because one of these does not put the whole truth before us, He gives us the two half-truths joined in one double parable (John 10). . . . Here, again (Acts 28:26-27) is God judicially inflicting blindness; and, on the other hand, men closing their own eyes. These two aspects of one awful truth are never far separated in the Word of God, often found side by side through the entire Book." (Emphasis his. *The Believer's Life; Its Past, Present, and Future Tenses,* pp. 24-26,30,16)

Since Presbyterians have been referred to, one more

source might be cited, and that an unusual one. Nathan L. Rice studied theology at Princeton, held various Presbyterian pastorates, and taught in that denomination's theological institutions. From all of that a strong Calvinistic emphasis would be expected. He wrote a book, published by the old Presbyterian Board of Publication (Philadelphia), the very title of which is most significant: *God Sovereign and Man Free.* In it he said: "All these passages teach with perfect clearness the free agency and accountability of man, and the sovereignty of God in bringing to pass His wise purpose. Men form their plans, and form them freely; but God bounds, overrules, and directs. . . . I might multiply, to any extent, examples of events certainly foreordained, yet brought to pass by the free and accountable agency of men. . . . It is certain that the decrees of God are not inconsistent with man's free agency. . . . We have seen, that God . . . can so govern even wicked men as to fulfill His purposes without interfering with their freedom of choice. . . . It is clear, therefore, that the decrees of God do not interfere with the free agency of men. . . . Every man is a free moral agent, perfectly free to accept or reject the offer of salvation. . . . The atonement, we believe, is sufficient to save all, if they would only believe; all are free moral agents, and may accept or refuse the offer of life. The gospel may, therefore, be sincerely offered to all, while they may be left to their own choice." (pp. 46,77,83,117-119)

Returning to a better-known name, Dr. G. Campbell Morgan, in a sermon on Hebrews 3:7-8, firmly spoke out: "Two things are assumed by the Holy Spirit in this text: first, that human responsibility begins with the hearing of the voice, 'today if ye shall hear His voice, harden not your hearts'; and, secondly, that when the voice is heard man is left free to obey or to disobey. . . . We cannot study this Bible without being brought face to face with personal responsibility. . . . A man in his choosing must choose definitely between right and wrong, light and darkness, good and evil. . . . The second assumption of this text is that of the freedom of the will when the voice speaks, 'Today if ye shall hear His voice, harden not your hearts.' This assuredly means that we can harden them if we will; we can disobey, we can see the light and choose the darkness; we can gaze on the high and admire it, and then turn our face to the depths. It is equally true that the heart can yield, that there can be obedience. . . . Responsibility is created by the voice of God; when the voice of God speaks, man's will is free to obey or to disobey." (*Westminster Pulpit,* Vol. VII, pp. 304,306-307)

In a work of a different nature, Dr. Morgan put further emphasis on the human will: " 'And ye would not!' That is the very heart of sin—'Ye would not'; the human will set up against the will of God. The human will set up against the will which had interpreted righteousness, and had expressed to men God's desire for human happiness and blessedness. . . . This was His purpose, 'I would'; and this was their sin, 'Ye would not.' . . . The action of these men had been willfully wicked. . . . Their inward pollution was of choice. 'Ye would not.' At last that attitude must work out its own issue." (*The Gospel According to Matthew,* fifth edition, pp. 279-280)

F. B. Meyer, the British Baptist whose books have blessed multitudes, gave full credit and glory to God, yet he did not neglect the human side. He is on record as saying: " '*Wilt* thou be made whole?' The whole question turns on the attitude of the will. And it is for lack of realizing this that many grope for years in darkness, who might otherwise walk in the light of life. . . . His [God's] one complaint against us is that we are *not willing.* 'Ye *will not* come unto Me, that ye might have life.' 'If any man *will* come after Me.' 'I would . . . but ye *would not.*' 'If ye be *willing* and obedient, ye shall eat the good of the land.' . . . His one prime concern is the will. What *willest* thou? *Wilt* thou be saved? The question of salvation is a moral one; it hinges on the will. . . . The initial step of salvation is our willingness to be saved." (Emphasis his. *Christian Living,* pp. 85,89-90,94)

In another work, Dr. Meyer says: "Come up out of the

wilderness, in which you have wandered so long. Your sojourn there has been due, not to any desire on the part of God, or to any arbitrary appointment of His, or to any natural disability of your temperament; but to certain grave failures on your part, in the regimen of the inner life." (*The Way Into the Holiest,* p. 67)

Another great Baptist preacher of Britain, Alexander Maclaren, has left us his superb *Expositions of Holy Scripture,* in which he wrote: "Obedience is in our power to give or to withhold. . . . God's grace constrains no man, and there is always the possibility open that when He calls we refuse, and that when He beseeches we say, 'I will not.' . . . But the practical point that I have to urge is this: There are two mysteries, the one that men *can,* and the other that men *do,* resist Christ's pleading voice. . . . If I cannot trust my sense that I can do this thing or not do it, as I choose, there is nothing that I can trust. Will is the power of determining which of two roads I shall go, and, strange as it is, incapable of statement in any more general terms than the reiteration of the fact; yet here stands the fact, that God, the infinite Will, has given to men, whom He made in His own image, this inexplicable and awful power of coinciding with or opposing His purposes and His voice. . . . Men do consciously set themselves against the will of God, and refuse the gifts which they know all the while are for their good." ("The Acts" II, pp. 333-334)

Again, this keen expositor of the Word said: "We are brought face to face with that strange and most inexplicable and yet most certain and tragic of all facts in regard to men, that they do turn away their wills from the merciful call of God, and that some of them, gnawing their very tongues with thirst, yet put away with impatient hand the sparkling cup that He offers to them freely. There is nothing sadder, there is nothing more certain, than that we poor little creatures can assert our will in the presence of the divine lovingkindness, and can thwart, so far as we are concerned, the council of God against ourselves. 'How often would I have gathered,' said the foiled, long-suffering Christ—'How often would I have gathered . . . and ye would not!' Oh! brethren, it is an awful thing to think that with this universal need there is such a partial yielding of the will to Him. . . . 'Whosoever will,' that is all. If you choose you may. No other conditions are laid down. If there had been any which were beyond the power of every soul of man upon earth, then Christianity would have dwindled to a narrow, provincial, sectional thing." ("Revelation," pp. 395-396,397. For similar emphasis read his striking sermon, "Thwarting God's Purpose," on Luke 7:30)

W. B. Riley, recognizing the sovereignty of God, also set forth his position on the freeness of the gospel and man's freeness in responding thereto: "The impression that prevails with some people that God only calls a few of His favorites is absolutely false. Isaiah, speaking for God, said, 'Ho, every one that thirsteth, come ye to the waters.' . . . No man ever hears the gospel, no matter who he is and to what stock he belongs, but God is calling to him. . . . Every promise of salvation made by the Son of God is His call to the sinner. . . . The soul's election depends upon the soul's choice. Thou, my friend, art the only person who can settle this question of election. It is not settled in Heaven; it is settled on earth. It is not settled of the Lord; it is settled by man." (*The Bible of the Expositor and the Evangelist* New Testament, Vol. 9, pp. 152-153,155,158)

Further emphasizing both aspects of the subject, the Baptist teacher and commentator, John A. Broadus, wrote: "From the divine side, we see that the Scriptures teach an eternal election of men to eternal life, simply out of God's good pleasure. From the human side, we see that those persons attain the blessings of salvation through Christ who accept the gospel invitation and obey the gospel commandments. It is doubtful whether our minds can combine both sides in a single view, but we must not for that reason deny either of them to be true." (*Commentary on Matthew*, p. 450)

In a little book by E. Y. Mullins there is a short chapter

on "Election," in which he said: "There are two choices necessary in a man's salvation: God's choice of the man and man's choice of God. . . . Salvation never comes otherwise than through God's choice of man and man's choice of God." Then, while pointing out the initiating part that God plays, he said: "Free will in man is as fundamental a truth as any other in the gospel and must never be canceled in our doctrinal statements. Man would not be man without it and God never robs us of our true moral manhood in saving us. . . . The decree of salvation must be looked at as a whole to understand it. Some have looked at God's choice alone and ignored the means and the necessary choice on man's part. . . . Arbitrariness and partiality in God is an error. God wills that all men should be saved and come to a knowledge of the truth (1 Timothy 2:4), as Paul assured us. Certainly Jesus died for the whole world (John 3:16)." (*Baptist Beliefs,* 4th ed., pp. 26-28)

A more recent book with a very similar title is *What Baptists Believe* by H. H. Hobbs. In it Dr. Hobbs said: "Man is endowed with free will, and thus he is responsible for his choices. He is not a pawn in the hands of fate. Nor is his conduct governed merely by physical forces apart from his will. Man is responsible to God for his acts. . . . The free will of man denotes man's freedom to act within the context of his own will and judgment. Otherwise, he would be nothing more than a puppet. . . . The doctrine of the free will of man appears to conflict with that of God's sovereignty. However, reason itself demands both, to say nothing of scriptural teaching. Both are facts of experience. The sovereignty of God must not cancel man's freedom, or else man loses his personality and is incapable of fellowship with God. God would become responsible for man's sin, a thought which is untenable with the very nature of God. . . . Man is free to receive or reject God's overtures of grace. But he is responsible for his response to them." (pp. 66-68)

Another recent book is *The Biblical Faith of Baptists,* Messages at the Fundamental Baptist Congress of North

America, Vol. I. The final message was given by Dr. Richard V. Clearwaters. The last page in this volume cites the position of Baptists: "To summarize the distinctions that the Baptist heritage, coming from the Ana-Baptists, has left throughout the ages we would say that they differ greatly and grossly with Covenant and/or Reformed Theology in their Biblical patterns and teachings on God's Decrees and Limited Atonement. . . ." (p. 224)

A much older book is one titled *Baptist Doctrines*, edited by C. A. Jenkens, a collection of notable essays and addresses (over 560 pages) on outstanding truths as held by Baptists. It contains, for example, C. H. Spurgeon's famous message on "Baptismal Regeneration." Among other contributors are Thomas Armitage, Wayland Hoyt, Alva Hovey, A. H. Newman, and A. J. Gordon.

For the chapter on predestination, a message was selected from the sermons of Richard Fuller of Baltimore, who had been educated at Harvard. Dr. Fuller's address begins by establishing the grounds for predestination and then goes on to free agency. The conclusion drawn is that both must be embraced: "In reference to predestination and free agency, there are two systems. . . . These schemes seem to our minds not only irreconcilable, but antagonistical. Yet the rejection of either involves us in consequences absurd and impious. And what is still more confounding, the Bible, with a directness and plainness admitting of no dispute or evasion, inculcates both of these conflicting doctrines. . . . It is impossible for us to reject either of these great truths. . . . I embrace both doctrines. Nay, more; I see clearly that if I reject either of these great truths and cling to the other, it will tow me away into fathomless depths of folly and impiety. . . . It is manifest that every call, every threat, every expostulation, every exhortation in the Bible supposes that man is a free agent. If he be not free, if he be the passive victim of inexorable, irresistible destiny, the Sacred Volume is a compilation of glaring inconsistencies—of sheer, downright falsehood and mockery." (pp. 495-497,502,493)

One more Baptist source might be quoted. Dr. O. C. S. Wallace wrote in his book, *What Baptists Believe: The New Hampshire Confession, An Exposition:* "We may confess that we cannot understand how the electing grace of God and a free-acting human soul sustain a consistent relation to each other in the realm of the freedom of each; but if we go beyond this confession, and deny that God elects, or that man is free, we shall plunge ourselves into greater difficulties than those from which we are seeking to escape. . . . We cannot observe man, acknowledge the human sense of responsibility, and yet deny to men freedom of choice." (p. 96)

Noted Scholars and Theologians Speak

Some may wonder whether, so far, we have not cited mostly popular preachers and writers; at least there may be a desire to know if students of the more technical aspects of the subject and those dealing with systematic treatments of theology concur in all of this. The witness of some of these may be observed.

Bishop H. C. G. Moule (Handley Dunelm) was both a deep student of the Word and a recognized scholar. He wrote: "Election never appears as a violation of human will. For never in the Bible is man treated as irresponsible. In the Bible the relation of the human and divine wills is inscrutable; the reality of both is assured. . . . Where election has been placed in the foreground of the system of religious thought, and allowed to dominate the rest, the truth has (to say the least) too often been distorted into an error." (Parenthesis his. *International Standard Bible Encyclopedia,* p. 927. See also under "Meaning of Election" following.)

Equally recognized for mental acumen and scholarship was Dean Henry Alford. In discussing these matters he said: "He willeth all to be saved, and that none shall perish except by *willful rejection* of the truth. So that, on the one side, *God's Sovereignty*—on the other, *Man's Free Will*—is plainly declared to us. To receive, believe, and act on both these, is our duty, and our wisdom. . . . We know as matter of fact, that in such cases not the divine, but the human side, is that ever held up by the apostle—the universality of free grace for all—the riches of God's mercy to all who call on Him, and consequent exhortations to all, to look to Him and be saved. The apparent inconsistencies of the apostle . . . resolve themselves into the necessary conditions of thought under which we all are placed, being compelled to acknowledge the divine sovereignty on the one hand, and human free will on the other. . . ." (*New Testament For English Readers,* Vol. II, Part I, "Romans," pp. 74, 78)

Marvin R. Vincent, a Presbyterian, was a noted theologian and linguist. He served Presbyterian pastorates and then became a professor in one of that denomination's theological seminaries. He translated from the Latin Bengel's *Gnomon of the New Testament,* but is best remembered for his volumes of *Word Studies in the New Testament* (utilizing the Greek). In the latter work he said: "That the factor of human freedom has full scope in the divine economy is too obvious to require proof. It appears in numerous utterances of Paul himself, and in the entire drift of Scripture, where man's power of moral choice is both asserted, assumed, and appealed to. . . . If human destiny were absolutely and unchangeably fixed by an arbitrary decree . . . the use of the divine promises themselves as appeals to repentance and holiness, the recognitions of the possibility of moral transformation, would assert themselves as a stupendous farce, a colossal and cruel satire. It must suffice for us that these two factors of divine sovereignty and human freedom are both alike distinctly recognized in Scripture." (Vol. III, pp. 136-137)

Dr. Archibald Alexander, another Presbyterian, was given by that group the task of organizing Princeton Theological Seminary. He was, as well, a professor, writer of numerous books, and widely recognized for his scholarship and gifts. The Baptist theologian, A. H. Strong, after referring to others in this area, says, "Archibald Alexander's statement is yet better," and then quoted him as follows: "Calvinism is the broadest of systems. It regards the divine sovereignty and the freedom of the human will as the two sides of a roof which come together at a ridgepole above the clouds. Calvinism accepts both truths. A system which denies either one of the two has only half a roof over its head." (A. H. Strong, *Systematic Theology,* p. 364)

Bishop Christopher Wordsworth* had some interesting words here, and then quoted no less than Augustine: "Nor does God's will overrule or constrain the freedom of man's will. God gives grace freely, in order that man may use his freewill rightly. Hence we find many appeals made to man in Scripture for the exercise, and right exercise, of his will.

"As Augustine says (the most earnest assertor of the power of divine grace)–In order that God may be willing to give, you must lend your will to receive. How can you expect that grace will fall upon you, unless you open the lap of your will to receive it? God gives not His righteousness without your will. Righteousness is only His. And volition is only yours. God's righteousness exists independently, without your will, but it cannot exist in you, against your will. Unless our will is in our power, it is not will." (Parenthesis his. *The New Testament in the Original Greek, with Introduction and Notes,* "Romans," p. 249)

Dr. W. H. Griffith Thomas was cofounder of the Dallas Theological Seminary. He was balanced in his teaching. In his commentary on Romans he wrote: "These two truths, God's Sovereignty and Man's Responsibility, are to be believed firmly, held tenaciously, proclaimed fully, and our life to be lived in the light thereof." (*Epistle to the Romans,* Vol. II, p. 155) Earlier Dr. Thomas quotes the continental scholar,

*Since we present citations from Dr. Wordsworth more than once hereafter, it might be said that he was the nephew and biographer of the poet William Wordsworth, himself an English medalist for poetry, received honorary degrees from both Oxford and Cambridge universities, was headmaster of Harrow, canon and then archdeacon of Westminster, Hulsean Lecturer at Cambridge, etc. The four volume Schaff-Herzog encyclopedia (Supplement, p. 243) lists by name 76 titles of his published works, many titles more than one volume, and some having gone through eight and nine editions.

Godet, as saying, "Has not the freedom of man its place in the course of history in perfect harmony with God's sovereign freedom in His acts of grace as well as His judgments?" (p. 149)

Considering things from the theological point of view, Dr. Thomas similarly expressed himself: "Divine grace is seen to be the source, support, and crown of salvation. And yet Scripture is equally clear and emphatic on human freedom and responsibility. Both sides are to be emphasized without any attempt at reconciliation. We must not isolate either the divine or the human side and consider one apart from the other. . . . The one thing to remember is that there is no favoritism with God and no injustice, nor is there any interference with the freedom of man or the universality of the offer of the gospel to human faith." (*The Principles of Theology*, p. 251)

Then in a note Dr. Thomas quoted Canon Liddon (of which observe especially the last part): "To us they seem like parallel lines, which must meet at a point in eternity, far beyond our present range of view. We do know, however, that being both true, they cannot really contradict each other, and that in some manner which we cannot formulate, the divine sovereignty must not merely be compatible with, but must even imply the freedom of created wills." (p. 252)

The last two quoted came from the Church of England. Some Baptist theologians have well expressed themselves on these matters.

Dr. E. Y. Mullins was president and professor of systematic theology in the Southern Baptist Theological Seminary of Louisville, Kentucky. In his work on theology, he said: "Can we reconcile the sovereignty of God and human freedom in His electing grace? The answer is in the negative. We are dealing here with ultimate forms of experience and of thought. God's sovereignty held in an abstract way and apart from our freedom, or man's freedom held in an abstract way apart from God's sovereignty, is a very hurtful and dangerous teaching. We are conscious of freedom as an ultimate fact of experience. We are driven to God's sovereignty as an ultimate necessity of thought. . . . God is limited by human freedom.

He made us free. He will not coerce man in his choices. If He did so He would destroy our freedom. We would cease to be persons and become things." (*The Christian Religion in Its Doctrinal Expression*, pp. 347-348)

Again, earlier in the same book, he said: "God's providential control of the world respects human freedom. Man is distinguished from physical nature by the possession of free personality. . . . God has limited Himself in His methods with free beings. Here compulsion is out of the question. Sovereignty and predestination do not annul freedom. If they did so, man would be reduced to the physical, or at least to the brute, level." (p. 268)

Another Baptist, this time from the North, may be cited. Dr. Nathan E. Wood was president of the Baptist school then known as Newton Theological Institution. He was later associated with or taught in Gordon College of Theology and Missions in its earlier days. To quote: "It seems as necessary to conserve and safeguard a true human freedom, if there is to be any human responsibility, as it is rightly to conserve divine sovereignty. Salvation is a transaction in which two free moral agents are concerned, and it is necessary that the quality in freedom, which is essential to make freedom real, shall not be overstated because it is in God, nor understated because it is in man. Freedom in God is independent. Freedom in man is dependent, but in each case that particular element must be conserved which carries with it responsibility. . . . Whatever loss or ruin has been wrought by sin in the moral nature, the remainders of that nature, which are essential to moral responsibility, still persist. Man acts, and is responsible as a moral being. There are diversities in his moral character. These surely spring from his own free moral choices. God . . . created men free moral beings. He certainly is a right judge as to whether or not such condition is derogatory to His sovereignty. This allows a rational and fair view of human freedom. It safeguards that freedom, and does not allow it to be crushed or become meaningless under divine sovereignty." (*The Person and Work of Jesus Christ*, American Baptist Publications Society, 1908, pp. 130-131)

It is appropriate to quote the late Henry C. Thiessen, who, with his Baptistic convictions, after being chairman of the Graduate School of Wheaton College, taught in a Baptist seminary. We read: "God has a very high regard for freedom. He could have made the creature an automaton, but He preferred to make him capable of choosing whether or not he would obey and serve Him. . . . God graciously restores to all men sufficient ability to make a choice in the matter of submission to Him. This is the salvation-bringing grace of God that has appeared to all men. . . . We dare not distinguish between a general call to all and a special call to the elect. Nor need we decide whether God's general call is sincere and His special call is irresistible. God does not mock men. If He offers salvation to all, then He also desires to save all, and to extend the same help to all who choose Him. Man's will is the only obstacle to the salvation of anyone. God does not give one man the will to do good and leave the other without all help in this respect." (*Lectures In Systematic Theology,* pp. 155,345,350)

Dr. A. C. Gaebelein has been well known as a writer of Biblical expositions, doctrinal and prophetic books, and he was for many years appreciated as editor of *Our Hope* magazine. His name appears along with that of A. T. Pierson, James M. Gray, William L. Pettingill, and others on the title page of the (old) *Scofield Reference Bible* as one of the consulting editors. He also left testimony on the subject before us. Commenting on John 5:40 he said: "Then follows that saddest of all words, 'Ye will not come unto Me, that ye might have life.' What a word this is! It gives us the solemn reason why men are lost. The Greek is more emphatic than the English version; it is more than 'Ye will not come'; it means literally rendered, 'Ye do not will to come.' After hearing His wonderful testimony, the different witnesses He had marshalled, they still refused to believe on Him, and had no heart and no desire to come to Him to receive that life which He alone can give." (*The Gospel of John,* p. 113)

While giving full recognition to the sovereignty of God and to salvation being wholly of grace, Dr. Gaebelein also said: "What He is and what He gives must be appropriated, and that is accomplished by coming to Him, and believing on Him. To come to Christ is to believe on Him, and to believe on Him is to come to Him. Both expressions mean that act of the soul whereby, under a sense of its sins and necessity, it flees to Christ, lays hold on Christ, trusts in Christ, and casts itself on Christ. . . . That God wants all men to be saved and is not willing that any should perish shows that hyper-Calvinism, which claims that God has foreordained a part of the human race to eternal damnation, cannot be true. . . . He will receive every one who cometh to Him; He will in nowise cast out those who have believed on Him. All may come to Him; all are invited to come and those who do come are received and kept by Him." (pp. 126,128)

Dr. Gaebelein was once asked to comment on a very pronounced Calvinistic book, A. W. Pink's *The Sovereignty of God,* in this question submitted to *Our Hope* magazine: "Do you think Mr. Pink's book, *The Sovereignty of God,* is scriptural? I recently read this book and it has upset me as no other book I ever read. I was attacked by terrible doubts as to God's justice and His very Being!"

Dr. Gaebelein's strong reply followed: "Mr. Pink used to be a contributor to our magazine. His articles on *Gleanings on Genesis* are good, and we had them printed in book form. But when he began to teach his frightful doctrines which make the God of Love a monster we broke fellowship with him.

"The book you have read is totally unscriptural. It is akin to blasphemy. It presents God as a Being of injustice and maligns His holy character. The book denies that our blessed Lord died for the ungodly. According to Pink's perversions He died for the elect only.

"You are not the only one who has been led into darkness by this book. Whoever the publisher is, and whoever stands behind the circulation of such a monstrous thing has a grave responsibility. It is just this kind of teaching which makes atheists." (*Our Hope,* Vol. 37, No. 11, May 1931, p. 684)

CHAPTER 2

THE HUMAN SIDE: ITS PLACE AND LIMITS

In what has gone before, it is seen that wide recognition is given to man's will. However, in reference to it and the free exercise thereof, several things are taken for granted as understood, and should be kept in mind throughout.

The Will Real, But Circumscribed

First, it is accepted that man's will is circumscribed in its exercise, that it operates within very definite limits, that it is bounded by the overall controlling plan and purpose of God, that the divine sovereignty is supreme in the larger outreach of all things. (Illustrations will be given later.)

Secondly, it does not mean that man, by the exercise of will, can of himself do that which will meet the just demands of a holy God, or that by anything that he does he can attain standing before God. Man in his fallen state cannot by any means please God nor do anything to save his own soul. Apart from the grace of God, man would be wholly and forever lost.

Thirdly, the employment of that free will which man does make use of is nothing meritorious, it is nothing wherein to glory or boast, it is nothing to his personal credit.

Fourthly, God, to be sure, has taken the first step in man's salvation by providing the Saviour, as planned in the eternal past. In His grace He furthermore provides the availability of that salvation to men through such means as the preaching of the gospel and through the convicting work of the Holy Spirit.

With these considerations in mind it may be noted that it

also seems clear that, to be saved, man must do something in the sense of exercising faith, believing the gospel, actively receiving the Saviour, and he will be held accountable if he does not do so; yet, as said, his exercise of that faith is nothing meritorious.

The reason why it is emphasized that faith has no merit, is so that, when it is urged that man must give heed to exercising faith, no objection can rightly be raised. That is, it cannot be claimed that salvation thereby ceases to be wholly of grace or that it is of human achievement, for the faith man exercises is entirely nonmeritorious, nothing which gives him the slightest ground for any claim on God. Faith, as will be seen, is the mere channel, not the ground of man's salvation. The ground or basis of salvation from sin, of course, is the divine provision in the finished work of Christ; the means or instrument of making effective that heavenly boon is an unworthy person casting himself on God's mercy and accepting it all for himself. This he must do, and he alone can do.

Faith Necessary, But Nonmeritorious

That man must receive salvation by faith and that his so doing would still not make it a matter of human achievement or of worthiness on his part, is evident in these quotations about the necessity of exercising faith, the freeness thereof, and the nonmeritorious nature of that faith.

Dr. Griffith Thomas said: "There is no credit or merit in the act of believing, for trust in another is absolutely incompatible with self-righteousness and dependence on our own powers. . . . Faith is an essential principle of human life, without which there can be no salvation. . . . There is absolutely no virtue or merit in faith. Trust is man's answer to God's truth. Faith is the condition, not the ground of salvation." (*Epistle to the Romans,* Vol. 1, pp. 154,165)

Similarly, Dr. E. Y. Mullins wrote: "We are not saved by works, but by grace through faith as the condition. Faith, then, according to the New Testament, is never regarded as a meritorious work. . . . Saving faith is an active as well as a passive principle. Looked at from one standpoint, faith is simply opening the hand to receive. It is simply surrender of the will. . . . Faith on man's part is not a work of merit possessing purchasing power, but the condition of salvation. Only by faith, apart from meritorious deeds, could man be saved." (*The Christian Religion in its Doctrinal Expression,* pp. 373,375-376)

Dr. Leander S. Keyser, whom H. A. Ironside characterized as "a great theologian,"* said on this: "Faith has been made, in Scripture, the channel through which justification comes to man for the very reason that it will exclude all human merit, and make man's salvation a pure work of God's grace. . . . From the very nature of faith it can have no merit. Faith is simply the act of the soul by which it accepts God's gift of salvation. There surely can be no merit in a poor, unworthy, guilty sinner accepting the grace which God gratuitously offers him. The fact is, the necessity of simply accepting the gratuity, without the ability to do anything to make him deserving, accentuates and enhances his unworthiness." (*Election and Conversion,* pp. 26-27)

Bishop H. C. G. Moule expressed himself on this in the following words: "Let us note that Faith, seen to be reliance, is obviously a thing as different as possible from merit. No one in common life thinks of a well-placed reliance as meritorious. It is right, but not righteous. . . . The man who, discovering himself, in the old-fashioned way . . . to be a guilty sinner, whose 'mouth is shut' before God, relies upon Christ as his all for pardon and peace, certainly does not merit anything for closing with his own salvation. He deserves nothing by the act of accepting all." (*The Fundamentals,* Vol. II, p. 116)

Several Baptist writers give brief but pointed testimony along this line. Dr. O. C. S. Wallace wrote: "Salvation comes to the soul that comes to salvation. Forgiving Saviour and penitent sinner meet. . . . The man cannot save himself . . . but he can lay hold by faith of the arm that is extended to

*H. A. Ironside, *In the Heavenlies,* p. 33.

save. . . . Because this salvation is of grace the saved man may not boast. . . . He paid no part of the price of his redemption; therefore he cannot boast of his resources." (*What Baptists Believe,* pp. 98-99)

In another book, W. R. White said: "Each must repent and believe; each must act in his own sovereign power of choice. The individual not only must act for himself; he is the only one who can. God has made him competent. It is not an inherent qualification of merit, but it is a divinely bestowed right based upon the mercy of God." (*Baptist Distinctives,* pp. 24-25)

This same truth was recognized by C. H. Spurgeon, who said, "A knowledge of the truth teaches us that faith is the simple act of trusting, that it is not an action of which man may boast; it is not an action of the nature of a work, so as to be a fruit of the law." (*Treasury of the New Testament,* Vol. III, p. 784)

Dr. A. T. Pierson put it this way: "When voluntary sin has been committed by a child of Adam, voluntary faith must enter into salvation. Insofar as any human being sins for himself, he must believe for himself. . . . Boasting is excluded. I have only to believe; this is my only work, the work of *faith*, which is my bond of union with the Justifier—to take Jesus as Saviour, to put on Christ, to accept the white robe of His perfect righteousness, which is 'unto all and upon all . . . that believe.' " (*The Believer's Life,* pp. 20, 33)

Dr. H. Clay Trumbull, founder and for many years editor of the *Sunday School Times,* pointedly said: "Hardly any single injunction is more frequently expressed by the Saviour of men, to those who desire His help, than the command to 'have faith in God.' It is their faith that Jesus insists on. It is on their faith that His help depends. It is by means of their faith that they are saved. So clearly and positively is this truth expressed in the Bible that those who would be guided by the precepts of that Book are ever ready to give prominence to the duty of faith as their ground of hope." (*How to Deal with Doubts and Doubters,* p. 51)

Dr. Albertus Pieters was a scholar and writer of the Reformed Church in America, a decidedly Calvinistic group, yet even he had a very strong testimony in this area: "We are not to think that since we are saved by faith, therefore faith is something meritorious. Faith is like the act of a beggar in stretching out the hand to receive my gift. He does not earn anything by that, not a cent; it is merely the acceptance of a free, unearned alms. . . . So there is no power in faith to save; the power is in Christ and His atoning work, but we cannot receive it without the touch of faith. . . . We know also that we are free and responsible beings, rejecting Christ, if we reject Him, because we have no love for holiness; and accepting Him, if we accept Him, of our own free will, without being in any way forced to do so." (*Facts and Mysteries of the Christian Faith,* third edition, pp. 167,185)

Another one from the Reformed Church in America was Dr. David James Burrell, whose published works were widely accepted. He said: "It does not devolve upon me to reconcile the divine sovereignty with freedom of the human will. . . . I am persuaded that there is an omniscient God; and I am equally sure that I have a sovereign will. The important fact is this: if I am ever saved, it will be by the exercise of personal faith; yet will I join with the innumerable company of the redeemed in ascribing all the glory to God." (*Old Time Religion,* pp. 336-337)

In this connection Dr. H. C. Thiessen quoted Dr. Hodge, of similar theological position to the two just quoted: "A positive response to prevenient [antecedent] grace is not 'merit.' Even Hodge said: 'There is no merit in the asking or in the willingness, which is the ground of the gift. It remains a gratuitous favor; but it is, nevertheless, suspended upon the asking.' " (*Lectures in Systematic Theology,* p. 157)

"Total Depravity" and "Inability"

A problem, however, may here present itself. Is not the total depravity of man recognized as an established precept of sound Biblical doctrine? And if so, how could man who is *totally* depraved—utterly sunk in sin and morally bankrupt—fulfill any responsibility at all in the matter of his own salvation?

Man, to be sure, *is* totally depraved. Before God he is wholly corrupt, utterly vile and filthy, steeped in sin and undone.

But as has often been pointed out, total depravity in man does not mean his total inability.

Dr. James Orr, the noted Scotch Presbyterian, said on this: "The doctrine in question is, indeed, misunderstood when the adjective 'total' is held to imply that every human being is as bad as he can be, or that there are not natural virtues, and even beautiful and lovable traits in characters that are yet unregenerate. . . . 'Total' here does not mean that every part of man is as corrupt as it can be, but that no part has escaped depravation or corruption (*totus,* in the sense of 'in every part'). Sin is in the nature, and its perverting, depraving, defiling influence pervades it all." (*Side-Lights on Christian Doctrine,* p. 97)

Dr. Griffith Thomas similarly wrote: " 'Total depravity' does not mean the absolute loss of every vestige of good, but that evil has affected every part of the nature and that nothing has remained untouched. . . . Free will means the freedom of the soul in choosing, enabling it to determine conscious action. . . . In this sense our freedom is real and the Fall has not affected it. . . . Fallen man has the faculty of will, as he has other faculties. . . ." (*The Principles of Theology,* pp. 165,180)

Coming to some Baptist theologians, we get various detailed comments. Dr. E. Y. Mullins said in part: "The phrase 'total depravity' has been employed in theology to describe the sinful state of men. But it needs careful defining lest it lead astray. In brief, it means that all the parts of our nature have been affected by sin. It does not mean that men are as bad as they can be, nor that all men are equally bad. It does not mean that human nature is destitute of all good impulse in the moral sense. It means rather that human nature, as such, and in all its parts in its unregenerate state, is under the dominion of sin. . . . Man is sometimes declared to possess 'natural,' but not 'moral' ability in things religious. By natural ability it is meant that he possesses all human faculties and powers, including will and the power of contrary choice. He is self-determined and not compelled in his actions. He is responsible and free. He is guilty when he does wrong. . . . On the other hand, it is asserted that man lacks 'moral ability' because he cannot change his own nature. . . . As we have defined these phrases both are true. . . . If a man is told that he has 'natural ability' in religious things, he is likely to overlook his dependence on God's grace. If he is told that he lacks 'moral ability,' he is in danger of losing his sense of responsibility." (*The Christian Religion in Its Doctrinal Expression,* pp. 294-295)

A. H. Strong showed what depravity is not, then what it is, and then said: "Yet there is a certain remnant of freedom left to man. The sinner *can* (a) avoid the sin against the Holy Ghost; (b) choose the less sin rather than the greater; (c) refuse altogether to yield to certain temptations; (d) do outwardly good acts, though with imperfect motives; (e) seek God from motives of self-interest. . . . The sinner can do one very important thing, *viz.,* give attention to divine truth." (*Systematic Theology,* p. 640)

In line with the last thoughts, Dr. H. C. Thiessen declared: "We believe that the common grace of God also restores to the sinner the ability to make a favorable response to God. In other words, we hold that God, in His grace, makes it possible for all men to be saved. . . . Paul says: 'For the grace of God hath appeared, bringing salvation to all men' (Titus 2:11). This results in the freeing of the will in the matter of salvation. That the will has been so freed is implied in the various exhortations to turn to God (Proverbs 1:23; Isaiah 31:6; Ezekiel 14:6; 18:32; Joel 2:13-14; Matthew 18:3; Acts 3:19), to repent (1 Kings 8:47; Matthew 3:2; Mark 1:15; Luke 13:3,5; Acts 2:38; 17:30), and to believe (2 Chronicles 20:20; Isaiah 43:10; John 6:29; 14:1; Acts 16:31;

Philippians 1:29; 1 John 3:23)." (*Lectures in Systematic Theology*, pp. 155-156)

Is Faith the Gift of God?

Another related point may naturally come up here. While the necessity of faith is recognized, still is not faith itself the gift of God?

It is true in one sense that faith is the gift of God, but it is God's gift to all who want it, to all who are willing to use it. Since, as is most generally agreed, the sincere offer of salvation is made to all, and since "whosoever will" may receive the gospel, it is evident that saving faith is within the reach of all. Such faith is given of God to those who desire to be saved. It is not given to all, because all will not avail themselves of it, will not yield to the moving of the Holy Spirit, and will not let the regenerating power of God work within them.

On the freeness of the gift of faith, Dr. R. A. Torrey said: "Faith is God's gift. Like all of God's gifts it is at the disposal of all who wish it, for there is no respect of persons with Him. We shall see directly that it is given through a certain instrument that is within reach of all, and upon certain conditions that any of us can fulfill." (*What the Bible Teaches*, p. 379)

Dr. William Evans said: "God wills to work faith in all His creatures, and will do so if they do not resist His Holy Spirit. We are responsible, therefore, not so much for the lack of faith, but for resisting the Spirit who will create faith in our hearts if we will permit Him to do so." (*The Great Doctrines of the Bible*, p. 149)

Similarly, Dr. Harry Ironside said: "Faith is the gift of God. . . . All men may have faith if they will; but alas, many refuse to hear the Word of God, so they are left in their unbelief. The Holy Spirit presents the Word, but one may resist His gracious influence. On the other hand, one may listen to the Word and believe it. That is faith. It is God's gift, it is true, because given through His Word." (*Full Assurance,* pp. 98-99)

Dr. C. I. Scofield put it somewhat differently: "There are three things, grace, faith, salvation, and these are all the gift of God. But here is the significant fact, dear friends, here begins your responsibility: of this wonderful trio—grace, faith, salvation—you have already received the gift of faith. Now you are saying: 'If I have faith, if already God has given me faith, why am I not saved?' Because you have not used it rightly—that is all. . . . Dear friends, do not make difficulties about things where there are no difficulties. Faith is a gift and you have it." (*In Many Pulpits With C. I. Scofield,* pp. 90-91)

Statements of C. H. Spurgeon point in the same direction: "As far as we can tell, faith has been selected as the channel of grace because there is a natural adaptation in faith to be used as the receiver. Suppose that I am about to give a poor man an alms: I put it into his hand—why? . . . The hand seems made on purpose to receive. So, in our mental frame, faith is created on purpose to be a receiver: it is the hand of the man, and there is a fitness in receiving grace by its means. . . . Both forgiveness and repentance flow from the same source, and are given by the same Saviour. . . . Jesus has both ready, and He is prepared to bestow them now, and to bestow them most freely on all who will accept them at His hands." (*All of Grace,* pp. 58,99)

Quite properly, then, Dr. H. C. Thiessen said, "It would seem very strange if God should call upon all men everywhere to repent (Acts 17:30; 2 Peter 3:9) and believe (Mark 1:14-15) when only some may receive the gift of repentance and faith." (*Lectures in Systematic Theology,* p. 349)

In view of these and other statements which seem to put a measure of responsibility for faith on man, what is the meaning of Ephesians 2:8, which reads, "For by grace are ye saved through faith; and that not of yourselves: it is the gift of God"?

Bible students, both recent and older, refer the "that not of yourselves," to the whole matter of being saved, not to the faith.

Thus, F. F. Bruce of England, said: "The fact that the demonstrative pronoun 'that' is neuter in Greek (*tauto*), whereas 'faith' is a feminine noun (*pistis*), combines with other considerations to suggest that it is the whole concept of salvation by grace through faith that is described as the gift of God. This incidentally, was Calvin's interpretation." (*The Epistle to the Ephesians,* pp. 51-52)

Similarly, A. T. Robertson said: " 'Grace' is God's part, 'faith' ours. *And that* (*kai tauto*). Neuter, not feminine *tautē*, and so refers not to *pistis* (feminine) or to *charis* (feminine also), but to the act of being saved by grace conditioned on faith on our part. Paul shows that salvation does not have its source in men, but from God." (*Word Pictures in the New Testament,* Vol. IV, p. 525)

M. R. Vincent succinctly said, "*And that.* Not faith, but the salvation." (*Word Studies in the New Testament,* Vol. III, p. 376)

W. E. Vine wrote on the use of "gift" here: "of salvation by grace, as the gift of God, Ephesians 2:8." (*Expository Dictionary of New Testament Words,* Vol. II, p. 146)

J. A. Smith, in the *American Baptist Commentary* on "Ephesians," wrote: "The Greek word for 'that' is neuter, so that the reference cannot be to 'faith,' since in that case it would be feminine. What is meant is the fact stated in the preceding clause." (p. 38)

Other students of the Word take a similar position. W. G. Blaikie, in the *Pulpit Commentary,* on "Ephesians," said: "On the part of God, salvation is by grace; on the part of man, it is through faith. . . . The grammatical structure and the analogy of the passage favor the former view, 'Your salvation is not of yourselves.'. . . Usage confirms the view that it is not merely faith, but the whole work and person of Christ which faith receives, that is meant here as the 'gift of God.' " (p. 63)

So also, Dean Alford said: " 'By grace' expressed the objective instrumental condition of your salvation—this 'through faith' the subjective medial condition: it has been effected by grace and apprehended by faith; *and this* ('your salvation,' your having been saved, as Ellicott) not of yourselves . . . the gift, viz., of your salvation." (Parenthesis his. *New Testament for English Readers,* Vol. II, Part I, p. 376) The more popular expositor, Alexander Maclaren, puts it this way: "Mark the last words of my text—'that not of yourselves: it is the gift of God.' They have often been misunderstood, as if they referred to the faith which is mentioned just before. But that is a plain misconception of the apostle's meaning, and is contradicted by the whole context. It is not faith that is the gift of God, but it is salvation by grace. That is plain if you will read on to the next verse. . . . What is it that is 'not of works'? Faith? certainly not. . . . The two clauses necessarily refer to the same thing, and if the latter of them must refer to salvation by grace, so must the former." (*Expositions of Holy Scripture,* "Ephesians," pp. 104-105)

Sir Robert Anderson put it even more strongly: " 'The gift of God' here is salvation by grace through faith. Not the faith itself. 'This is precluded,' as Alford remarks, 'by the manifestly parallel clauses "not of yourselves," and "not of works," the latter of which would be irrelevant as asserted of faith.' It is still more definitely precluded, he might have added, by the character of the passage. It is given to us to believe on Christ, just in the same sense in which it is given to some 'also to suffer for His sake' (Philippians 1:29). But the statement in Ephesians is doctrinal, and in that sense the assertion that faith is a gift, or indeed that it is a distinct entity at all, is sheer error. The matter is sometimes represented as though God gave faith to the sinner first, and then, on the sinner's bringing Him the faith, went on and gave him salvation! Just as though a baker, refusing to supply empty-handed applicants, should first dispense to each the price of a loaf, and then, in return for the money from his own till, serve out the bread! To answer fully such a vagary as this would be to rewrite the following chapter. Suffice it, therefore, to point out that to read the text as though faith were the gift, is to destroy not only the meaning of verse 9, but the force of the whole passage." (*The Gospel and Its Ministry*, thirteenth edition revised, p. 54 footnote)

The whole matter may finally be pointed up in the words of no less a person than Washington Gladden, who said, "What says the text? 'By grace are ye saved through faith; and that not of yourselves: it is the gift of God.' But a tyro in Greek knows that the pronoun translated 'that' cannot refer to faith, and must refer to salvation by grace. Read the next verse. 'Not of works, lest any man should boast.' What is not of works, faith, or salvation? To say that faith is not of works, is nonsense; to argue that salvation is not of works, is to do just what Paul is doing. The grace of God, the pardon and sympathy and help of God, is God's free gift; it is nothing that we have earned or merited; it is gratuity.... The act of accepting salvation is surely man's act, and that act is faith. The free act of God in bestowing salvation is grace; the free act of man in accepting it is faith." (*A Homiletic Encyclopaedia*, R. A. Bertram, editor, p. 342)

CHAPTER 3

THAT TO WHICH PREDESTINATION AND ELECTION REFER

At this point the question may naturally arise, how then are predestination and election to be understood? For an answer we do not have far to go. The answer is so simple it is amazing that so many have stumbled over it. Predestination and election do not refer to certain people of the world becoming saved or lost, but they relate to those who are already children of God in respect to certain privileges or positions out ahead; they look forward to what God will work in those who have become His own. This is seen in the works of a number of outstanding men of God.

Most of those who treat the general subject take predestination and election in very much the same sense, but since a few make a technical distinction, we will take up first predestination and then election, also showing what some say about the whole matter in general.

Predestination

As to predestination, Dr. H. A. Ironside showed the limited use of that term in the Bible: "Turn to your Bible and read for yourself in the only two chapters in which this word 'predestinate' or 'predestinated' is found. The first is Romans 8:29-30. The other chapter is Ephesians 1:5,11. You will note that there is no reference in these four verses to either Heaven or hell, but to Christlikeness eventually. Nowhere are we told in Scripture that God predestinated one man to be saved and another to be lost. Men are to be saved or lost eternally because of their attitude toward the Lord Jesus Christ. Predestination means that some day all the redeemed shall become just like the Lord Jesus! Is not this precious? Do not try to make a bugaboo out of that which was intended to give joy and comfort to those who trust the Saviour. Trust Him for yourself, and you will know that God has predestinated you to be fully conformed to the image of His Son." (*Full Assurance,* pp. 93-94)

In another work, one of an expository nature, Dr. Ironside said: "It is the Father who has predestinated us to the adoption of children. Nowhere in the Bible are people ever predestinated to go to hell, and nowhere are people simply predestinated to go to Heaven. Look it up and see. We are chosen in Christ to share His glory for eternity, but predestination is always to some special place of blessing. Turn to Romans 8:29. Predestinated to what? Predestinated 'to be conformed to the image of His Son.' You see, predestination is not God from eternity saying 'This man goes to Heaven and this man to hell.' No, but predestination teaches me that when I have believed in Christ, when I have trusted Him as my Saviour, I may know on the authority of God that it is settled forever that some day I am to become exactly like my Saviour." (*In The Heavenlies,* Expository Addresses on Ephesians, pp. 34-35)

Sound scholarship sees the future element in this. For example, the great Greek authority and prominent Baptist, Dr. A. T. Robertson, wrote on Romans 8:29, ". . . to express the gradual change in us till we acquire the likeness of Christ the Son of God so that we ourselves shall ultimately have the family likeness of sons of God. Glorious destiny." (*Word Pictures in the New Testament,* Vol. IV, p. 377)

Another who referred to the original text was the honored Baptist pastor and writer, Dr. I. M. Haldeman: "There are great facts concerning us as believers which relate us to the dispensation of the fullness of times. . . . He has predestinated us to the place of sons in that dispensation, as it is written (Ephesian 1). . . . The expression, 'the adoption of children,' in the Greek is *uiothesia*. . . . The compound word, therefore, signifies 'son placing—the place of a son.' Thus, as believers, we have been predestinated in that coming dispensation to the place of sons." (*The Book of the Heavenlies,* pp. 4-5)

Again, on this general aspect of things, Dr. W. L. Pettingill wrote: "Whosoever will may come. He is only to come, and God does all the rest. God will . . . undertake for him, and thereafter see to it that all things work together for good unto him. This is His eternal purpose which He purposed before the world was. . . . The word 'for,' in [Romans 8] verse 29, has the force of 'because,' and it introduces the reason for our assurance that all things are working together for our good. . . . The past tense continues through the whole passage, although the glorification is yet future, for God is able to count things done even when they have not been done. Our glorification is according to His purpose, and nothing is to be suffered to thwart His purpose. Having been foreknown and predestinated and called and justified, we shall also be glorified." (*Bible Questions Answered,* third edition, p. 374)

Even C. I. Scofield said briefly (on Romans 8:28-30), "Then follows another revelation of truth for the stay of suffering saints; we are in a process the end of which is sure. That end is absolute conformity to Christ." (*Scofield Bible Correspondence Course,* Vol. II, p. 275)

Dr. W. B. Riley explained the matter this way: "The term 'predestination' which has alarmed many, is only another expression of the eternal compassion, the eternal plan, the eternal purpose, the eternal project—redemption. The believer's position, however, is by the exercise of man's will. He has 'predestinated us unto the adoption of children by Jesus Christ to Himself, according to the good pleasure of His will'; but He will never foreclose on that which He has purchased without our personal consent. The day one is willing to be adopted, that day he becomes God's child. . . . Our adoption is done the moment we consent to it; but the joy of it all, to the praise and glory of His grace—comes to us in ever-increasing measure." (*The Bible of the Expositor and the Evangelist,* N. T. Vol. 12, pp. 13-15)

On this Dr. Herbert Lockyer said: "Predestination is the exercise of divine sovereignty in the accomplishment of God's ultimate purpose.... What must be borne in mind is the fact that predestination is not God's predetermining from past ages who should and who should not be saved. Scripture does not teach this view. What it does teach is that this doctrine of predestination concerns the future of believers. Predestination is the divine determining the glorious consummation of all who through faith and surrender become the Lord's." (*All the Doctrines of the Bible,* p. 153)

C. H. Spurgeon, apparently seeing the point in this, said: "Mark then, with care, that OUR CONFORMITY TO CHRIST IS THE SACRED OBJECT OF PREDESTINATION.... The Lord in boundless grace has resolved that a company whom no man can number, called here 'many brethren,' shall be restored to His image, in the particular form in which His Eternal Son displays it.... Now, therefore, the one thing to which the Lord is working us through His Spirit, both by providence and by grace, is the likeness of the Lord from Heaven." (Capitals his. *Treasury of the New Testament,* Vol. II, p. 72)

A more recent Baptist, one who studied under some notable Baptist leaders and who for some years taught in one of the nation's largest Baptist training schools, is Mark G. Cambron. He stated: "Scripture teaches that God has predestinated those who have believed (and who will believe) to be conformed to the image of His Son. In other words, it is the plan of God, determined beforehand, that every believer is going to be made like unto the Lord Jesus Christ.... God has determined that those who are saved are going to be like His Son." (*The New Testament—A Book-by-Book Survey,* pp. 200-201)

Similarly clear and positive testimony comes from a beloved pastor whom those who knew regarded as a godly character and forceful preacher of the Word, Pastor Edward Drew of the Madison Avenue Baptist Church of Paterson, New Jersey, whose Sunday messages were broadcast, and many taken down and put in printed form: "People have had it drilled into them that away in the past God foreordained that certain people should be lost and certain others should be saved. I would like to get that out of your minds this morning. Just let me begin by saying that that isn't in the Bible.... God's predestination is not salvation. God's predestination is that those who receive the Lord shall be like the Lord Jesus. That is predestination, and nothing else is. God from the beginning, by His foreknowledge, predestinated that every believer should be made like Christ, and nothing else in the Book is predestination. That predestination is that God ordained one to be saved and another to be lost in hell eternally is not within the covers of this Book.... God has ordained from the foundation of the world that if you will trust His Son, He will make you like His Son. That is what we have here.... Those whom God predestinated to be like Christ, He called out—not before He saved them, but when He saved them, He called them out to be like Him.... It isn't that in the past God called you and didn't call somebody else. God's predestination is being worked out now. In eternity past He determined that you should be like Jesus, and now that you are saved He calls you out, that while you are here you should show forth the Lord Jesus Christ." (Message delivered Sunday morning, March 1, 1942, on Romans 8:29-32)

Election and What It Involves

Coming to the term *election,* here also there has been a jumping to conclusions. Some theologians may feel impelled, basing their reasonings on philosophy, to bring it into a rigid system which attempts to explain everything from beginning to end. But that such postulates are the only explanations does not by any means follow. It can be seen in the view of many well-known writers that election largely involves: (a) the community or body as a whole (individuals as comprising the body); (b) it has to do with service or witness to the world as part of the plan of God; and (c) it looks less back than forward to what lies out ahead for those called of God. In addition, the word *elect* is taken by some to be more of a title and it may refer to individuals as related to position, privileges, or office. The following excerpts bring out various aspects of the subject.

Dr. H. C. G. Moule said of election: "It is always (with one exception, Romans 9:11; see below) related to a community, and thus has close affinity with the Old Testament teachings upon the privileged position of Israel as the chosen, selected race. The objects of election in the New Testament are, in effect, the Israel of God, the new, regenerate race called to special privilege and special service. . . . It is assumed there (2 Peter 1:10) that the Christian, baptized and a worshiper, may yet need to make 'sure' his 'calling and election' as a fact to his consciousness. This implies conditions in the 'election' which far transcend the tests of sacred rite and external fellowship." (*International Standard Bible Encyclopedia,* p. 925)

In *What Baptists Believe,* H. H. Hobbs set forth the subject as follows: "The word 'election' does not appear in the Old Testament and is found in only six verses of the New Testament. The word 'elect' appears four times in the Old Testament and sixteen times in the New Testament. The word translated 'elect' is sometimes rendered 'chosen.'. . . Election is not mechanical. It involves a God who is love and a man who is morally responsible. It never appears in the Bible as a violation of human will. . . . When reduced to its simplest elements election is twofold. First, God elected a plan of salvation which He accomplished in Christ. Man may either reject this plan or accept it. . . . Secondly, God elected a people to make known His elected plan of salvation. . . . Thus election is to both salvation and evangelism. In both, the free will of man determines the final result. By free will men can elect to be saved but elect to be barren Christians.

God forbid! Men can also elect to be both saved and fruitful Christians." (pp. 106-107)

Dr. Frederic W. Farr was pastor of Calvary Baptist Church in Los Angeles and was also the first professor of theology at the Los Angeles Baptist Theological Seminary. He said: "The purpose of God in redemption is comprehensive and far-reaching. . . . The various elections of God, like that of the Jews or even of the Church, are not for their own sakes alone, but as a means to an end. This view does away with the common cavils against election. The purpose of God . . . seeks and secures the greatest possible good in the aggregate." (*A Manual of Christian Doctrine,* p. 103)

Dr. W. H. Griffith Thomas put it this way: "The outcome and purpose of this selection is seen in the service which God intends the elected man or nation to render. . . . St. Paul is concerned not so much with individuals, as with nations and masses of people. He speaks of God's choice of Israel, not to eternal life as such, but to the privilege and duty of receiving His grace in order to work for and with Him for the establishment of His kingdom. . . . God's chosen men are His 'choice' men, and all through Scripture His choice men . . . endure hard, strenuous sacrificing service on behalf of others." (*Epistle to the Romans,* Vol. II, p. 229)

Dr. H. H. Rowley is a widely recognized British scholar, professor, and author. His background is Baptist. A few years ago he delivered a series of lectures in Spurgeon's College, London. He referred to his great debt to Charles Haddon Spurgeon. His addresses were published as *The Biblical Doctrine of Election.* The foremost thrust of the book is to show that election has to do with the service of God and witness to the world, whether of Israel or the Church, and the responsibilities entailed for those who enter the sphere involved.

Having dealt extensively with the election of Israel, Dr. Rowley turned to the Church, saying: "In the teaching of the New Testament the Church is the elect, and the Church consists of those who have yielded themselves to the power of Christ, and to His obedience. . . . The Church is elect because it is the company of the elect. . . . Every one who belonged to the fellowship of the Christian Church was thought of as elect." (pp. 168-170)

And very extensive is his demonstrating that election is to service: "Whom God chooses, He chooses for service. There is variety of service, but it is all service, and it is all service for God. . . . The divine election concerns exclusively the divine service. . . . Election is for service. This is not to ignore the fact that it carries with it privilege. For in the service of God is man's supreme privilege and honor. . . . To those who willingly and consciously accept the task to which they are called, the resources of God are open for the fulfillment of their mission, and here again is high privilege. Yet it is never primarily for the privilege but for the service that the elect are chosen. . . . Their election is for service, and it is only valid insofar as, and so long as, they fulfill that purpose. . . . The complaint against the Biblical doctrine of election, that it is unjust, is here more than anywhere shown to be beside the mark. For what is commonly meant by the complaint is that it is unjust that the elect should be favored. It has been insisted throughout these lectures that while there is favor and honor in being chosen by God, His election has always its reverse side in the service it involves. But here it would appear that if there is injustice, it is directed against the elect and not in his favor. His is a heritage of suffering. . . . Always election and response in service and loyalty belong together, and the final repudiation of the service is equally the renunciation of the election. . . . They who fail to respond are the evidence that election does not really turn man into a puppet and sweep away his will." (pp. 42,45,111,117-118, 120)

Robert Tuck, another scholarly British writer, in the second of his two large volumes of *Bible Difficulties,* has some words on "The Divine Election": "What we can plainly see in the divine dealings with races, nations, families, and individuals, is a divine selection of some for special forms of service in relation to, and for the benefit of, the others. . . . The endowments, or the dispositions, of the nation or the individual, fit them, in the divine arrangement, for that particular place of service. . . . From this point of view it becomes clear that God's election concerns disposition and endowment, and consequently position and service. But the divine election should never be so presented as to assume that it relates to character or to destiny." (*A Handbook of Biblical Difficulties,* second series, p. 472)

Similarly, Dr. James Orr said: "There is the divine 'election'; but electing love, one comes to see, is never election to the exclusion of others, but election with a view to the future larger blessings of others." (*Sidelights On Christian Doctrine,* p. 34)

Again, the end of election in service is brought out by F. B. Meyer: "The Hebrew nation was marvelously privileged. . . . But these privileges were granted, not for the nation itself, but for the blessing of mankind. This is the meaning of election. There are elect races, elect nations, elect souls, that they may be able to impart of what they have received, and communicate whatever advantages have been intrusted." (*Through The Bible Day by Day,* Vol. VI, p. 88)

Equally pointed are the words of Sanday and Headlam in their scholarly work on Romans, in an excursus designated "The Divine Election": "The thought again and again recurs that Israel has thus been chosen not merely for their own sake but as an instrument in the hand of God, and not merely to exhibit the divine power, but also for the benefit of other nations." (*International Critical Commentary,* "Romans," p. 249)

Dr. M. G. Cambron declared: "The words 'chosen' and 'election' have to do with the purpose of God in service. Israel was that chosen nation which God used to preach the Kingdom of God to the world. . . . The Church is that nation through whom God is now preaching the Kingdom of

God. . . . The only requisite to become the called of God is faith." (*The New Testament, A Book-by-Book Survey,* p. 201,203)

M. R. Vincent, a Presbyterian and an authority on Biblical languages, is on record thus: "*Eklogē* election, this, and the kindred words, *to choose,* and *chosen* or *elect,* are used of God's selection of men or agencies for special missions or attainments; but neither here nor elsewhere in the New Testament is there any warrant for the revolting doctrine that God has predestined a definite number of mankind to eternal life, and the rest to eternal destruction. . . . Election—the act of God's holy will in selecting His own methods, instruments, and times for carrying out His purposes—is a fact of history and of daily observation." (*Word Studies in the New Testament,* Vol. IV, p. 16; Vol. III, p. 137)

Another testimony may appropriately take its place here. Sir Robert Anderson, while well known among the Plymouth Brethren, was actually affiliated with the English Presbyterians. He was known generally to take the Calvinist position. His works went through many editions. From the thirteenth edition, revised, of one of his works is this quote: "The scriptural expression 'God's elect' . . . like 'first born,' is a title of dignity and privilege, applicable exclusively to the Christian. The prominent thought in election, especially in this dispensation of the *Church* (as the very word *ecclesia* suggests), is rank and privilege, not deliverance from perdition. . . . The theological doctrine based upon it is too often pressed beyond the limits of the positive teaching of Holy Writ. . . . It is not that He has grace for the elect and judgment for all beside. . . . It is not that there is mercy for a favored class, but that there is mercy, and nothing else, for all without distinction. . . . If forgiveness is preached to all, it is because all may share it." (*The Gospel and Its Ministry,* pp. 76,85-86)

Dr. H. A. Ironside had this to say: "D. L. Moody used to put it very simply: 'The elect are the "whosoever wills"; the nonelect are the "whosoever won'ts." ' This is exactly what

Scripture teaches. The invitation is to all. Those who accept it are the elect. Remember, we are never told that Christ died for the elect." (*Full Assurance,* p. 92)

Again, Dr. Ironside said, " 'Whosoever' means *whosoever.* Only a biased theologian with an ax to grind could ever think that it meant only the elect." (*What's The Answer?* p. 35)

In his work on theology, Dr. E. Y. Mullins said: "Does God's election coerce man's will, or does it leave it free? The answer is emphatically that the will of man is not coerced, but is left free. In his free act in accepting Christ and His salvation man is self-determined. He would not have made the choice if left to himself without the aid of God's grace. But when he chooses, it is his own free act. . . . Grace does not become effective until men freely respond to it." (*The Christian Religion in Its Doctrinal Expression,* pp. 344-345)

Another Baptist writer, C. L. Daniel, put it this way: "The doctrine of unconditional election does indeed make God a respecter of persons. In fact it is . . . a tenet quite foreign to the Holy Writ. It takes one of the Lord's sweetest and most gracious teachings and turns it into the most heartless and tyrannical, by making God Himself directly responsible for the doom of every lost sinner." (*The Bible's Seeming Contradictions,* p. 45)

Pastor Edward Drew brought out the practical side thus: "The subject of election, as it is in the New Testament, is not what a lot of folks think it to be. Election in the New Testament is not that God formerly, in the past ages, determined to save one man and take him to Heaven, and send another man to hell. That is not in the Bible. . . . God has said [in effect], 'My elect are those who believe what I say.' They are the elect. . . . How do you get to be one of the elect? God determined, in the far ages of the past, that He would have a select people who would be made up of those who believe His Word. And whosoever will may come and believe, and be one of God's select and elect company. You can make your calling and election sure; and if you have believed God, and know you are saved, you know you are one of the elect. Beloved, that is election as you have it in the

New Testament." (Studies in First and Second Thessalonians, message, September 12, 1943)

On the forward look, or the goal to be seen in election, the following statements further touch that element. Dr. F. B. Meyer said: "Notice to what we are elect. We are elect to obedience. Not merely that we should escape the penalty due to sin. . . . Elect to be nearest Christ, because resembling Him most closely in ministry, and devotion, and love. . . . We are chosen to obey; to serve; to learn; to suffer; to die daily—that others may be blessed and saved. . . . There is a divine purpose which is pledged to carry us onwards to beauty of moral character and an obedience which is fashioned after the pattern of Christ's." (*Tried by Fire*, pp. 12-13)

Somewhat similarly Dr. Nathan E. Wood said: "Men, both bad and good, are selected not to salvation nor reprobation, but for their uses toward the preparation of that final universe which is to be ultimately realized. . . . Selection may be racial, national, or family, without including every individual and without implying that it was a choice to eternal life. . . . Selection for the carrying forward of a divine purpose is not, then, necessarily an election to eternal life. . . . It is not difficult to discover what is the ultimate purpose of God in election. . . . His purpose runs through all created things to a final social order, in which righteousness shall have natural, sole, and undisputed regnancy. God's election ensures this." (*The Person and Work of Jesus Christ*, pp. 122-123,127)

In a work by H. C. G. Moule different from the one previously cited, the author said on this aspect of the subject, "The elect are the Church. . . . Bright is their prospect in His plan; it is nothing less than the 'eternal glory' of His presence above; He will love them, He will keep them, even to the end." (*The Second Epistle to Timothy, Devotional Commentary*, p. 84)

No less scholarly a work than the *International Critical Commentary*, said: "Here what is chiefly in view is not the fact of 'selection,' but the end for which the choice was made. . . . The condition of faith is implicitly contained. Every man who by faith accepts the call is *eklektos.*" (T. K. Abbott, on Ephesians 1:4, p. 6)

In the little book by E. Y. Mullins before quoted from, the author closed his short section on election with these words: "All uncertainty vanishes in the full persuasion, warranted by the Scriptures, that God guides, controls, and efficaciously wills the glorious outcome." (*Baptist Beliefs,* p. 29)

This section may fittingly be closed by quoting from some who show what both predestination and election basically involve.

H. H. Hobbs said: "Predestination . . . simply means that God has predetermined that those who respond affirmatively to His call or election will be justified, or declared righteous, and furthermore will be glorified. All of this is 'according to His purpose.'. . . God's sovereign will elects those who are to be His 'royal priesthood' and 'holy nation' for the salvation of all men. The free will of man either accepts or rejects this relationship. . . . God has elected salvation to all who, in freedom of will, will call on Him or who will meet the conditions of the elected plan of salvation. In short, God has provided in His election all that is necessary for man's salvation." (*Fundamentals of our Faith,* pp. 94,98-99)

On this general theme, Oliver B. Greene said: "If God has everything cut and dried–elected and chosen–predestinated and fixed–why on this earth did Jesus request the disciples to pray that more laborers would be sent into the fields white unto harvest? If some are elected to Heaven while others are not–If some are predestinated and others are not–If some are chosen for salvation and others are not–Why did the Lord Jesus say, 'Even so it is not the will of your Father which is in heaven, that one of these little ones should perish' (Matthew 18:14)?. . . The Church as a body was chosen in the beginning by Almighty God. The Church as a body was chosen to be the Bride of Christ. As a body it was chosen, elected, and predestinated to be a holy Church without spot or wrinkle. Paul is not suggesting that some are chosen to be saved and others are elected to go to hell." (*Presdestination,* pp. 19,28)

The late Dr. William G. Coltman, pastor of a great Baptist church in the Detroit area, told the story of a man who, when appealed to by a preacher, gave the objection, "Well, if I am one of the elect I will be saved anyway, and if not, there is nothing I can do about it." Whereupon the preacher said, "God 'now commandeth all men every where to repent' [Acts 17:30]. God's commands are enablings, and if you will hearken you will be saved. But you will not dare say in that day, 'I could not, because I was not one of the elect,' for that would not be true. The reason you refuse to come would be found in your love of sin, not in your nonelection." (*Cathedral of Christian Truth,* p. 238)

(See also in Part II the treatment of these terms in such texts as Romans 9, Ephesians 1, and 1 Peter 1, where they are dealt with further.)

CHAPTER 4

GOD'S SOVEREIGNTY IN RELATION TO FREE WILL

A question may arise at this point. It seems that if God be God, He must be supreme, absolutely sovereign in His universe. All is working out under His control, and according to His plan. If that be the case, how could man have any measure of independent action?

Man Controlled or Free?

In many of the sources which have been quoted, there have been declarations regarding man having free will. But where, in a rigidly controlled universe, is there any room for free or independent action on the part of a finite creature? If everything, in its totality and its most minute detail, is in the firm grip of a Supreme Being, and He directs the affairs of men, is man in his every act merely following out a prefixed course? Is his assumed free will only an illusion, something which he thinks he possesses, but which in reality has no basis in ultimate fact?

Some deep thinkers on this subject have concluded that both concepts are true: that it is a noble view of God to see Him in His supremacy voluntarily allowing man a certain limited sphere of free action. Of course it would only be within the circle of man's own circumscribed existence that this is granted, beyond which God remains in absolute control. By the nature of the case, man's actions would be bounded in many ways and only exercised within the sphere allotted to him by his Creator. To allow man such a measure of self-determination is something which only a great and omnipotent God would do. The greater and more supreme

He is (coupled with the greatness of His grace), the more He would willingly grant man such restricted freedom of action. Anything short of that would result in a merely mechanical universe, a world of rigid determinism. Furthermore, such a mechanistic existence would leave no room for real human responsibility or accountability, or ground for a final judgment, nor would it allow place for any spontaneous response to one's Maker. A little reflection will raise the question, why under such conditions of prefixation would God reason with men or plead with them, why call upon men to repent and turn from sin, why express grief over man's refusal to heed his Maker?

It should be borne in mind that if allowing man a measure of freedom were imposed upon God from without, or if it were forced upon Him by some strange necessity, objection to it might be made. But when it is that which He alone initiates—of His own voluntary doing—out of pure love and for high and lofty ends which His unmitigated omnipotence assures, it is only to the praise of His glory that it is so.

God's Voluntary Self-Limitations

To some it may seem nothing less than startling to suggest that even within some small area God would limit Himself or would withdraw from full direction of certain minute details, but note how it has been thought of.

Dr. William E. Biederwolf graduated from both Princeton University, and Princeton Theological Seminary, where in his senior year he won the Greek prize. He was a great preacher and writer, and for a number of years head of the Winona Lake School of Theology. He said: "Suppose we accept the explanation which affirms that God's foreknowledge and foreordination are not necessarily all-comprehending. You shrink from an attitude of thought like that toward the Supreme Being. It appears, does it not, to reflect discredit upon His perfection? Yet, let us not be too hasty in our judgment. Many earnest and noted scholars defend the position and strenuously maintain that not only does it not dishonor God, but that it is the only scheme of thought which does not divest Him of the essential attributes of His divinity."

Then Dr. Biederwolf applies the principle to the active relations between man and God, saying, if God "can, in response to the petition of His confiding child, alter what, without such petition, would have been otherwise, we find ourselves wondering if such a view is not, in comparison with that of absolute predestination, equally honoring to God and quite as stimulating to man. To many it seems far more so."* (*How Can God Answer Prayer?* third edition, pp. 113-114,120-121)

To quote again from Nathan E. Wood: "God is conditioned by the fact that there are human souls. It is not derogatory to His infinite sovereignty to say that He is conditioned in His relations with men, by the will of man. It is a condition which He chose to put upon Himself when He created men free moral beings. He certainly is a right judge as to whether or not such condition is derogatory to His sovereignty. . . . God acts omnipotently but always within limits which preserve man's moral freedom and responsibility." (*The Person and Work of Jesus Christ,* pp. 130-131,157)

E. Y. Mullins, who wrote on apologetics as well as theology, said: "God controls nature in accordance with laws. But man is on a higher level. God has limited Himself in His methods with free beings. . . . God is limited by human freedom. Again, God is limited in His methods by human sin. . . . God must reduce His own action to the minimum lest He compel the will. We conclude then, that God is limited by human freedom and sin to the method of election, and that in executing His purpose He must, by reason of these limitations, work gradually and through human agents." (*The Christian Religion in Its Doctrinal Expression,* pp. 268,348,349)

---

*Further data on this may be found in Appendix B, Dr. Biederwolf's citation from Kinsley.

Dr. Henry C. Thiessen declared: "God ... can foresee how men will act without efficiently decreeing how they shall act. God is not limited in the carrying out of His plans, except as He has limited Himself by the choices of man. ... God has set certain general bounds within which His universe is to operate. Within these bounds He has given man freedom to act." (*Lectures in Systematic Theology,* pp. 346,396)

H. E. Guillebaud wrote as follows: "When God created man with free will, the question arises how far He submitted Himself to the limitation of His own almighty power, so that the free will which He had bestowed should be allowed a real exercise. ... There are passages which seem to qualify the absoluteness of the divine sovereignty, by implying that human misuse of free will can nullify His gracious purposes. As an instance take our Lord's saying about the Temple (Mark 11:17). God's gracious purpose for the Temple, declared in His own inspired Word, is contrasted with the actual condition to which the Temple had been brought by human greed. Or take an example from the Old Testament. A man of God said to Eli, 'Jehovah ... saith, I said indeed that thy house, and the house of thy father, should walk before Me for ever: but now Jehovah saith, Be it far from Me; for them that honour Me I will honour, and they that despise Me shall be lightly esteemed' (1 Samuel 2:30). ... May it not be that, together with the final plan of God which must always prevail (because He is sovereign and also frames His plans in knowledge of the future), there is also a provisional purpose, which God would gladly have fulfilled for His creatures, which in human language we may say that He longs to fulfill, but which they are permitted to obstruct? This would explain all those places where God expresses His longing that His creatures would act in such a way as would make it possible for Him to bless them as He desires. ... The Bible depicts God as behind all human history, but so that the divine sovereignty does not rule out either free will or human sovereignty, but rather that He allows the absoluteness of His sovereign will to be qualified by the freedom of human choice." (*Some Moral Difficulties of the Bible,* Inter-Varsity Fellowship, 1941, pp. 60,65-66,75)

From the pen of Dr. Kenneth J. Foreman, professor of doctrinal theology in the Louisville Presbyterian Theological Seminary, comes a striking illustration and then a statement of position: "Let us imagine two horsemen. One sits on a horse every movement of which he controls absolutely. The horse does not move a fraction of an inch in any part unless the rider decides it shall so move and sees to it that the movement is made. Here we see absolute control. Another man sits on another horse. This horse makes various movements which the rider does not command, does not initiate, cannot even predict in detail. But the rider is in control. The first horse is a hobbyhorse; the second is a spirited five-gaited showhorse. But which is the better horseman? Little Willie, operating his mechanical horse in the corner drugstore, or the prize-winning rider at the horse show? Is it actually more to the credit of God that He shall ride this universe like a hobbyhorse, or like a real, living creature of intelligence and spirit? . . . We Christians will not give up believing in the sovereignty of God. We Presbyterians will not need to apologize for keeping that high truth central in our doctrine of God. But we do not have to suppose that God cannot be sovereign without robbing His creatures of all their freedom." (K. J. Foreman, *God's Will And Ours,* p. 30)

In *What Baptists Believe,* Dr. H. H. Hobbs wrote: "God . . . can do as He wills, said will being in accord with His nature which involves such attributes as His truth, holiness, righteousness, and love. In this sense God has placed certain limitations on Himself. He has willed not to violate the free will of man (Genesis 3). He does not act contrary to His own nature (Genesis 18:25). . . . God is sovereign in that He can do that which He wills and which is in accord with His nature. He is not only omnipotent; He is love. Furthermore, man, made in God's image, possesses free will." (pp. 16,106)

The learned Dr. C. Wordsworth touched upon it this way: "The display of God's *sovereignty* to the world is the *end* which He has in view. The *end* is always sure; for it is an end fixed by God. The *means* are left free to man. Men may choose the good, and they may choose the evil; they may obey God, and they may rebel against Him. This is by God's own permission; for He has given them free will. If they obey Him, as God desires and commands and invites them to do by many gracious promises of reward, then His glory is promoted directly by their actions. . . . Whether they obey Him or rebel against Him, the end which is His glory, is always attained. His design cannot be frustrated by their sin." (*The New Testament in the Original Greek, With Notes and Introductions,* "Romans," pp. 195-196)

Dr. A. T. Robertson very simply commented on 1 Timothy 2:4: "Who will have all men to be saved": "Willeth, God's wish and will insofar as He can influence men." (*Word Pictures in the New Testament*, Vol. IV, p. 567)

Another Baptist writer and recognized scholar, Dr. E. C. Dargan, said: "God is too great to be placed in opposition to man, as though they were equals; He includes man's choice in His choosing, man's work in His working. Man can be very comfortably free *within* the overwhelming purpose and operation of God." (*The Doctrines of our Faith,* revised edition, p. 129)

Earlier in the same work he said: "Human freedom is denied by fatalists and materialists; but surely, while we recognize the limitations of human freedom, we yet are conscious of power to choose within limits our own way, and conscious, too, of the responsibility of choice." (p. 78)

George W. Truett, in what is probably his most notable volume of sermons, said: "That is a striking expression used in one of the Psalms, where the Psalmist said, concerning Israel of old: 'They limited the Holy One of Israel.' They 'limited God.' Mankind can limit God and does limit Him. At first thought, that seems impossible. The infinite God, filling all immensity, without beginning of days or ending of years, omnipotent, omniscient, omnipresent, eternal–at first thought it seems impossible that He could be limited, and yet

He can be, and is, limited. Man limits God, else man is a mere machine, without any more volition than a tree or a stone. Man can say 'No' to God, or man can say 'Yes' to God. Man can seek God's face . . . or man can be rebellious. . . . We are told here in the Gospels that in one certain community Jesus could do no mighty works because of the unbelief of the people. Unbelief hindered Him. Unbelief fettered Him, even Christ Jesus, the Lord." (*A Quest For Souls,* pp. 33,35)

Man, therefore, is seen to possess a will which is real, and its use may be of momentous consequence, for God sovereignly allows man to resolve certain issues to his own weal or woe. But while recognizing this place of free will and responsibility in man, we know, of course, that God holds the reins of the universe in His firm grip. We also rest assured that with God in control evil will never triumph; that Satan himself can go only so far and no farther; that forces of iniquity will be finally and completely put down and judged. Likewise, we believe that God has a plan for each yielded life; that, as we allow Him to do so, God will work out His perfect will for each of us, and we do not need to walk in the light of our own eyes.

Suggested Illustrations

Sometimes an illustration serves to clarify things, and at this point some that have been suggested may prove helpful.

Dr. W. H. Griffith Thomas presented the following, which shows both the place of free choice and its limits: "As has been well pointed out, it is open to a man to choose whether he will or will not take poison, but if he takes it the result cannot be fixed by his own will; the power of God in the laws of nature settles the issue." (*Epistle to the Romans,* Vol. II, p. 155)

Dr. A. H. Strong in his *Systematic Theology* presented an illustration which is suggestive: "The man who carries a vase of goldfish does not prevent the fish from moving unrestrainedly within the vase." (p. 363) The man, the superior being in this case, keeps for the moment the goldfish bowl in a state of being moved. He may determine, unhindered, whether he will place the bowl on the table, on the window sill, or on the piano; near the light or in the shade; etc. If he is benevolent we may suppose that he will so act as to insure the best conditions for the goldfish. And his will is overruling. The fish themselves, however, within the well-defined limits of their bowl, have a measure of free choice. They may swim one way or another, or they may cease from all swimming and rest on the bottom of the bowl or float near the top of the water. As food is available, they may partake of little or much or none at all. The superior creature, man, does not force the food down their throats nor determine the exact amount which each individual fish will partake of. If the illustration be shifted to pets of a higher order, the man may urgently appeal to their cooperation for their own good and he may desire a degree of fellowship with them, but still, while superior, he does not control their every movement. Yet their apparently free liberty is circumscribed by the very sphere of their existence. In all of this there may be a thought as to how man may have a measure of free choice but not thereby vitiate the sovereignty of God.

Another illustration, this one from the writings of A. W. Tozer, was presented by Professor Robert Lightner. "A. W. Tozer gives this illustration of the relationship between divine sovereignty and human freedom: 'An ocean liner leaves New York bound for Liverpool. Its destination has been determined by proper authorities. Nothing can change it. . . . On board the liner are several scores of passengers. These are not in chains; neither are their activities determined for them by decree. They are completely free to move about as they will. They eat, sleep, play, lounge about the deck, read, talk, altogether as they please; but all the while the great liner is carrying them steadily onward toward a predetermined port. Both freedom and sovereignty are presented here, and they do not contradict each other. So it is, I believe, with man's freedom and the sovereignty of God. The mighty liner of God's sovereign design keeps its steady course over the sea of history. God moves undisturbed and unhindered toward the fulfillment of those eternal purposes which He purposed in Christ Jesus before the world began.' " (Regular Baptist Press Quarterly, *Doctrine of God,* Adult Student, pp. 29-30)

Misrepresentations

Since compiling the above, our attention has been drawn to a booklet on the sovereignty of God published in Kentucky. It purports to give statements on this theme by some of the great Baptists of the past. On the cover are pictured most of the Baptist leaders from whom quotations are cited. There occur, however, gross misrepresentations of certain of these men. For example, John A. Broadus is pictured, and then, within, three and one-half lines are quoted from his commentary on Matthew. It is amazing to find that these lines are from exactly the same passage which we quoted earlier, but only that part is given which seems to support rigid election. Broadus has qualifying statements both before and after the words quoted. The entire statement, which shows that he held to both sides of the question, as we contend, is as follows: "This selection of the actually saved may be looked at from two sides. From the divine side, we see that the Scriptures teach an eternal election of men to eternal life, simply out of God's good pleasure. From the human side, we see that those persons attain the blessings of salvation through Christ who accept the gospel invitation and obey the gospel commandments. It is doubtful whether our minds can combine both sides in a single view, but we must not for that reason deny either of them to be true." (*Commentary on Matthew,* p. 450) What a difference the last two sentences make!

Again, J. M. Pendleton is quoted from his book *Christian Doctrine.* True, he held to election, but note what he also believed, which is conveniently omitted in the Kentucky publication: "In God's purposes 'violence is not offered to the will of the creature.' There are no truths more plainly revealed in the Bible than that God is sovereign and man is free. . . ." Then, after giving the king of Babylon as an illustration, he said: "But the exercise of divine sovereignty does not conflict with human agency. It was, doubtless, among the purposes of God to make man a free agent. What is a free agent? I answer in the words of Andrew Fuller: 'A free agent is an intelligent being, who is at liberty to act according to his choice, without compulsion or restraint.' The question is not as to what prompts to action; the point is that the action is free. Men have acted freely in all ages of the world. The purposes of God, whether efficient or permissive, have not prevented such action. Good men have acted freely, and bad men have acted with equal freedom." (*Christian Doctrines,* pp. 103-104)

Pendleton quoted from Andrew Fuller, another whom this southern publication pictures and cites as though he were an outstanding sovereignty man. Yet Baptist history records that he was actually one of the strongest leaders against the rigid Calvinism of the day. Another southern publication, written by a Southern Baptist scholar, said of Fuller: "He was the determined foe of hyper-Calvinism. He said in his strong way, 'had matters gone on but a few years the Baptists would have become a perfect dunghill.' His work entitled: *The Gospel Worthy of All Acceptation,* was an epoch making book." (John T. Christian, *A History of the Baptists,* Vol. I, p. 351)

One who took a position in the opposite direction from Andrew Fuller was John Gill. The historian just quoted said of Gill: "He did not invite sinners to the Saviour, while preaching condemnation, and asserted that he ought not to interfere with the elective grace of God." This writer then referred to "the withering effect of such a system of theology." (pp. 347-348) The little booklet from the South quotes rightly from Gill.

Another Baptist historian records that the great Baptist preacher, Robert Hall, said of Gill's commentary, "a continent of mud, sir." (H. C. Vedder, *A Short History of the Baptists,* p. 240) Even C. H. Spurgeon, while recognizing his value, said of Gill: "The portrait of him . . . turning up his nose in a most expressive manner, as if he could not endure even the smell of free will. In some such vein he wrote his commentary. He hunts Arminianism throughout the whole of it . . . he falls upon a text which is not congenial to his creed, and hacks and hews terribly to bring the Word of God into a more systematic shape." (*Commenting and Commentaries,* Kregel edition, p. 9)

Again, while trying to appreciate Gill (Spurgeon became pastor of Gill's old church), Spurgeon said, "The system of theology with which many identify his name has chilled many churches to their very soul, for it has led them to omit the free invitations of the gospel, and to deny that it is the duty of sinners to believe in Jesus." (*Spurgeon's Autobiography,* Vol. I, p. 310)

Another testimony along these lines is in Dr. J. B. Jeter's book entitled *Baptist Principles Reset* (third edition). In his introductory chapter, after setting forth some widely recognized doctrinal points as held by Baptists, he said: "It may be proper to add that Baptists generally hold to what may be termed, for the sake of distinction, 'moderate Calvinism.' They are far from acknowledging Calvin as authority in matters of religion; but the system of doctrine which bears his name, as it has been modified by the study of the Scriptures, is now commonly accepted by Baptists. Fifty years ago [written in 1902], they mostly adhered to high Calvinism, as maintained by Dr. John Gill, of London. Since that time their views have been considerably changed, through the writings of Andrew Fuller and others." (pp. 12-13)

CHAPTER 5

C. H. SPURGEON'S OTHER SIDE

The position of the celebrated C. H. Spurgeon has often been appealed to. He made strong statements on the sovereignty of God. But those who stop there do not do justice to Spurgeon. To be sure, he emphasized the divine sovereignty, yet that is only one side of Spurgeon. A study of his works shows that he forcefully brought out the other side as well.

This is also the observation of some who knew Spurgeon well. Dr. Arthur T. Pierson was called upon to follow immediately the ministry of Spurgeon at the Metropolitan Tabernacle in London, where he carried on for several years. He must therefore have had a real acquaintance with and an understanding of Spurgeon's position. He recognized clearly the two sides of Spurgeon's outlook: "Divine sovereignty and human freedom are alternately emphasized in Scripture, and no attempt is made to harmonize them. The fault with all theological systems is that they attempt a scientific harmony and adjustment of what the Word of God leaves an unsolved problem and a hopeless paradox. C. H. Spurgeon had not long been a preacher and a pastor before he also was content to insist on God's sovereign election of man and on man's voluntary election of God, as both true and essential to salvation. But he made no more attempt to make them harmonize than Christ did before him, when He said almost with the same breath, 'No man can come to Me, except the Father which hath sent Me draw him,' and again, 'Ye will not come unto Me.' "(Pierson, A. T.: *Seed Thoughts For Public Speakers*, p. 271)

Dr. A. H. Strong in his *Systematic Theology* (p. 364), in coming to the problem of balancing the divine side by recognizing also the human side, referred, among others, to C. H. Spurgeon's *The Best Bread* (p. 109) in a sermon on the crucifixion: "The quaternion of soldiers did whatever they wished to do. They acted of their own free will, and yet at the same time they fulfilled the eternal counsel of God. Shall we never be able to drive into men's minds the truth that predestination and free agency are both facts? Men sin as freely as birds fly in the air, and they are altogether responsible for their sin; and yet everything is ordained and foreseen of God. The foreordination of God in no degree interferes with the responsibility of man. I have often been asked by persons to reconcile the two truths. My only reply is–They need no reconciliation, for they never fell out. Why should I try to reconcile two friends? Prove to me that the two truths do not agree. These two facts are parallel lines; I cannot make them unite, but you cannot make them cross each other. Permit me also to add that I have long ago given up the idea of making all my beliefs into a system. I believe, but I cannot explain. I fall before the majesty of revelation, and adore the infinite Lord."

Spurgeon expressed himself somewhat similarly in another sermon: " 'All that the Father giveth Me shall come to Me; and him that cometh to Me I will in no wise cast out' (John 6:37). These two sentences have been looked upon as representing two sides of Christian doctrine. They enable us to see it from two standpoints–the Godward and the manward. . . . The second sentence sets forth blessed, encouraging, evangelical doctrine, and is in effect a promise and an invitation–'Him that cometh to Me I will in no wise cast out.' This is a statement without limitation of any kind: it has been thought to leave the free grace of God open to the free will of man, so that whosoever pleases may come and may be sure that he will not be refused. We have no permission to pare down either sentence, nor is there the slightest need to do so. . . . These are two great truths; let us carry them both with us, and they will balance each other. I was once asked to reconcile these two statements, and I answered, 'No, I never reconcile friends.'... The grand declaration of the purpose of God that He will save His own is quite consistent with the widest declaration that whosoever will come to Christ shall be saved. The pity is that it ever should be thought difficult to hold both truths.... Take, then, these two truths, and know that they are equally precious portions of one harmonious whole." (*The Treasury of the New Testament,* Vol. II, p. 355)

Again, while still glorying in the divine side to which he gives full place, Spurgeon recognized the human side, even with its limitations: "That is a truth, about which, I hope, we have never had any question; we hold tenaciously that salvation is all of grace, but we also believe with equal firmness that the ruin of man is entirely the result of his own sin. It is the will of God that saves; it is the will of man that damns.... There are great deeps about these two points. The practical part of theology is that which is most important for us to understand. Any man may get himself into a terrible labyrinth who thinks continually of the sovereignty of God alone, and he may equally get into deeps that are likely to drown him if he meditates only on the free will of man. The best thing is to take what God reveals to you, and to believe that.... What is wanted is, first, the real will to come to God. You have heard a great deal, I dare say, about the wonderful faculty of free will.... There is where the sinner fails, what he needs is a real will.... There is no true willingness in your hearts, for a true willingness is a practical willingness. The man who is willing to come to Christ says, 'I must take away with my sins, I must away with my self-righteousness, and I must seek Him who alone can save me.' ... There is need of an immediate will. Are you willing to come to Christ now? That is the point.... So, you see, it is a real will and an immediate will that is needed." (*Treasury of the New Testament,* Vol. I, pp. 340,342)

Once more Spurgeon clearly expressed himself: "See how sweetly the second clause of our text puts it—'Whosoever will, let him take of the water of life freely.' Whether thou be thirsty or not, yet hast thou a will to drink? hast thou a will to be saved? a will to be cleansed from sin? a will to be made a new creature in Christ Jesus? Dost thou will to have eternal life? Then thus saith the Spirit to thee, 'Whosoever will, let him take of the water of life freely.' . . . 'Whosoever'—then what man dare have the impudence to say that he is shut out? If you say that you cannot come in under 'whosoever,' I ask you how you dare narrow a word which is in itself so broad, so infinite. 'Whosoever'—that must mean every man that ever lived, or ever shall live, while yet he is here and wills to come." *(Treasury of the New Testament,* Vol. IV, p. 845)

In another connection Spurgeon said: "You do not trust Him; you do not obey Him. I pray you account for the fact. 'May I believe Him?' saith one. Have we not told you ten thousand times over that whosoever will may take of the water of life freely. If there be any barrier it is not with God, it is not with Christ, it is with your own sinful heart. You are welcome to the Saviour now, and if you trust Him now He is yours forever. . . . You turn your back upon the incarnate God who bleeds for men, and in so doing you shut yourselves out of hope, judging yourselves unworthy of eternal life. . . . There is one water of life, but you refuse to drink it; then must you thirst forever. You put from you, voluntarily, the one only Redeemer; how then shall you be ransomed?" (*Treasury of the New Testament,* Vol. II, pp. 301,303)

In a sermon entitled "Human Responsibility," Spurgeon said: "I have often been rebuked by certain men who have erred from the truth, for preaching the doctrine that it is a sin in men, if they reject the gospel of Christ. I care not for every opprobrious title: I am certain that I have the warrant of God's Word in so preaching, and I do not believe that any man can be faithful to men's souls and clear of their blood, unless he bears his frequent and solemn testimony upon this vital subject. . . . I have not kept back the glorious doctrines of grace, although by preaching them the enemies of the cross have called me an Antinomian; nor have I been afraid to preach man's solemn responsibility, although another tribe have slandered me as an Arminian. And in saying this, I say it not in a way of glorying, but I say it for your rebuke, if you have rejected the gospel, for you shall have sinned far above any other men; in casting away Christ, a double measure of the fury of the wrath of God shall fall on you." *(Memorial Library,* Vol. V, pp. 426,429)

In a sermon on the text, "Compel them to come in," Spurgeon said: "I should be worse than a fiend if I did not now, with all love, and kindness, and earnestness, beseech you to 'lay hold on eternal life.' Some hyper-Calvinist would tell me I am wrong in so doing. I cannot help it. I must do it. As I must stand before my Judge at last, I feel that I shall not make full proof of my ministry unless I entreat with many tears that ye would be saved, that ye would look unto Jesus Christ and receive His glorious salvation."

In the same sermon, on a single double-column page, in his pleading Spurgeon seven times quoted verses with "whosoever" or "whoso" in them; " 'Whosoever believeth,' 'whosoever calleth upon,' 'whosoever cometh unto,' 'whosoever believeth,' 'Whosoever will, let him come,' 'Whoso calleth upon,' and 'Whosoever will.' " *(Treasury of the New Testament,* Vol. I, pp. 885,882)

In another work Spurgeon again set forth the freeness of human action: "Inanimate matter obeys the divine law by force, but a human being can only obey God with his will, since unwilling obedience would be no obedience at all. There can be no such thing as unwilling love, unwilling trust, or unwilling holiness. Voluntariness enters into the essence of a moral act. Having, therefore, so fashioned man, the Lord doth not forget this fact, but ever treats man as a free agent. The divine compulsions of His grace are only such as are congruous with a willing and nilling creature." *(Illustrations and Meditations, or Flowers From a Puritan's Garden,* p. 124)

From a different source comes another even stronger statement from Spurgeon: "Griffiths says that travelers in Turkey carry with them lozenges of opium, on which is stamped *'mash Allah,'* the gift of God. Too many sermons are just such lozenges. Grace is preached but duty denied. Divine predestination is cried up but human responsibility is rejected. Such teaching ought to be shunned as poisonous, but those who by reason of use have grown accustomed to the sedative, condemn all other preaching, and cry up their opium lozenges of high doctrine as *the truth,* the precious gift of God. It is to be feared that this poppy-juice doctrine has sent many souls to sleep who will wake up in hell." *(Feathers for Arrows,* p. 65)

To demonstrate more fully Spurgeon's emphasis upon the part to be played by man, his sermons, as for example, on certain texts in the Gospels, may be read. With fervent plea, he insists that the gospel is for all men, urges all to flee to the Saviour, and sets forth the peril they will be responsible for if they fail to act. In his sermon on 1 Timothy 2:4 he derides those who would turn "have all men to be saved" into "some men" or into "who will *not* have all men to be saved."

His autobiography has some interesting things. We read where another is quoted as saying of him: "He discoursed upon 'Human Responsibility.'. . . Not long afterwards he set forth both sides of divine truth in a sermon entitled 'Sovereign Grace and Man's Responsibility,' in which he avoided the errors of Arminianism on the one hand, and those of hyper-Calvinism on the other." *(Autobiography,* Vol. II, p. 224)

In the same work Spurgeon said of the students who went out from his Pastor's College: "Some few have ascended into hyper-Calvinism, and, on the other hand, one or two have wandered into Arminian sentiments; but even these have remained earnestly evangelical, while the bulk of the brethren abide in the faith in which their alma mater nourished them." The emblem of the Pastor's College was a hand holding the cross, to which were adjoined the words: "I Hold and am Held." *(Ibid.,* p. 150)

In *Spurgeon's Lectures to His Students,* edited by David Otis Fuller, it is evident that Spurgeon spoke with force and even with a bit of sarcasm to those who were going to labor in the gospel. In a chapter entitled, "On Conversion As Our Aim," he said: "Any and every appeal which will reach the conscience and move men to fly to Jesus we must perpetually employ, if by any means we may save some. . . . In our Master's name we must give the invitation, crying, 'whosoever will, let him take the water of life freely.' Do not be deterred from this, my brethren, by those ultra-Calvinistic theologians who say, 'You may instruct and warn the ungodly, but you must not invite or entreat them.' And why not? 'Because they are dead sinners, and it is therefore absurd to invite them, since they cannot come.' Wherefore then may we warn or instruct them? The argument is so strong, if it be strong at all, that it sweeps away all modes of appeal to sinners. . . . Who among the sons of men would think it a great vocation to be sent into a synagogue to say to a perfectly vigorous man, 'Rise up and walk'? He is a poor Ezekiel whose greatest achievement is to cry, 'Ye living souls, live.' " (pp. 327-329)

Consideration of Spurgeon's position may well be concluded by presenting what is recorded by a British scholar thoroughly versed in this area: "Charles Haddon Spurgeon always claimed to be a Calvinist. . . . His mind was soaked in the writings of the Puritan divines; but his intense zeal for the conversion of souls led him to step outside the bounds of the creed he had inherited. His sermon on 'Compel them to come in' was criticized as Arminian and unsound. To his critics he replied: 'My Master set His seal on that message. I never preached a sermon by which so many souls were won to God. . . . If it be thought an evil thing to bid the sinner lay hold of eternal life, I will yet be more evil in this respect, and herein imitate my Lord and His apostles.'

"More than once Spurgeon prayed 'Lord, hasten to bring in all Thine elect, and then elect some more.' He seems to have used this phrase often in conversation, and on his lips it was no mere badinage. With its definite rejection of a limited atonement, it would have horrified John Calvin. . . . The truth seems to be that the old Calvinistic phrases were often on Spurgeon's lips but the genuine Calvinistic meaning had gone out of them.

"J. C. Carlile admits that 'illogical as it may seem, Spurgeon's Calvinism was of such a character that while he proclaimed the majesty of God he did not hesitate to ascribe freedom of will to man and to insist that any man might find in Jesus Christ deliverance from the power of sin.' " (Underwood, A. C., *A History of The English Baptists,* pp. 203-205)

(See further statements of C. H. Spurgeon in various places in this work as listed in the Index.)

CHAPTER 6

FOREKNOWLEDGE, AND WHAT MAY BE FORESEEN

In the foregoing pages the term *foreknowledge* has not been mentioned. Foreknowledge, as frequently discussed, is a subject more of interest to theological students. Many writers tie it in with election, or the divine decrees, or predestination. Scripture briefly alludes to it, and since connected with this whole subject, it may be looked at for the sake of those who are interested.

A point commonly considered, as related to the destiny of men, is, does God extend His blessings of salvation to men because of something foreseen in certain ones, but which is not foreseen in others? Or, does God simply elect certain ones to salvation for no apparent reason, His infinite will alone being the total cause? And if the latter be the case, then to what does foreknowledge refer? Does it merely relate to those whom He had already determined to save?

Pronounced Calvinistic writers, laying great stress on the sovereignty of God, judge that it could not be anything foreseen in man which even remotely might be the basis of His acting in their behalf. He acts alone on His own inscrutable will. Taking this position, some naturally conclude that foreknowledge is an inexplicable mystery. Is such a general viewpoint necessary to give full glory to God? There are many on record who believe just the opposite; who believe that God is more exalted by recognizing some deeper truth here. It is not necessary to go to the extreme of Arminianism to take that position.

Some have gone so far as to raise the question: can God foreknow something without causing it? Those taking an extreme position, whose thinking is perhaps philosophically conditioned, have concluded that He cannot. They declare that foreknowledge is of a determinative nature. But if God foreknows everything, and foreknowledge is determinative, that of course would entail the conclusion that God has prefixed everything. And foreknowledge would cease to be foreknowledge in the commonly understood sense.

Many moderate Calvinists have pointed out that in salvation God does not base His foreknowledge on anything that man does in the way of good works; that it was not because of anything foreseen in man of merit, or of obedience to the law, or of upright character that God acted in favor toward any man. But, they insist, that is quite different from saying that God possibly foresaw in certain men the free exercise of nonmeritorious faith, a willingness to humble themselves in the dust before God, acknowledge their utter unworthiness and accept that which they could never in any way have come near to by themselves. And to such, He having foreknown their voluntary response, God gives, wholly in grace, the gift of Christ's purchased redemption.

In the following statements note how these things have been brought out, observing, for example, the distinction between foreseen merit and the foreseen response of unworthy men; how alien to foreknowledge would be the idea that it is determinative; and other elements that might be involved.

Dr. E. Y. Mullins said: "Does God choose men to salvation because of their good works or because He foresees they will believe when the gospel is preached to them? Beyond doubt God foresees their faith. Beyond doubt faith is a condition of salvation. The question is whether it is also the ground of salvation. The Scriptures answer this question in the negative. . . . Election is not to be thought of as a bare choice of so many human units by God's action independently of man's free choice and the human means employed." *(The Christian Religion in Its Doctrinal Expression,* pp. 343,347)

Dr. Griffith Thomas put the matter this way: "God's will

follows His knowledge and He foreordained them to be conformed to the image of His Son. . . . Though sovereign, the divine choice is never arbitrary, i.e., nonrational or nonmoral. . . . In [Ephesians 1] verse 11 we have 'the *counsel* of His own will.' This teaches us that His will is never arbitrary, but is based on reason. . . . While the apostle points out that God's exercise of sovereign choice is independent of man's physical descent or personal merit, he nowhere hints that the choice works independently of human character or choice. While mercy and judgment belong to God alone, He has clearly revealed the conditions under which He exercises His awful sovereignty. The Scriptures are full of statements as to the kind of people upon whom God wills to have mercy (Isaiah 55:7)." *(Epistle to the Romans,* Vol. II, pp. 96,135,144,152)

C. Wordsworth explained it this way: "They who abuse their free will and reject what He offers, and what He desires them to accept, shall fail of salvation, and incur punishment and perdition. . . . But in making this statement, we must not fall into the Arminian error, which represents man's goodness, foreseen by God, as the ground of God's predestination of the godly. . . . Man's faith in God is indeed a condition of that predestination, but God's love to man in Christ is its cause. . . . God's foreknowledge, though it foresees everything, forces nothing. He foreknows everything that will be; but nothing will be because He foreknows it." *(The New Testament in the Original Greek, With Notes and Introductions,* "Romans," p. 198)

Turning again to the Presbyterian, M. R. Vincent, we read on Romans 8:29: "*Did Foreknow.* Five times in the New Testament. In all cases it means *foreknow.* It does not mean *foreordain.* It signifies *prescience,* not *pre-election."* Then in a footnote, Vincent says: "The attempt to attach to it the sense of pre-election, to make it include the divine decrees, has grown out of dogmatic considerations in the interest of a rigid predestinarianism. . . . The infinitesimal hair-splitting which has been applied to this passage . . . is as profitless as it is unsatisfactory." *(Word Studies in the New Testament,* Vol. III, p. 95)

This writer said further: "A predetermination of God is clearly stated as accompanying or (humanly speaking) succeeding, and grounded upon the foreknowledge. This predetermination is to the end of conformity to the image of the Son of God. . . . Therefore, the relation between foreknowledge and predestination is incidental, and is not contemplated as a special point of discussion." *(Ibid.,* p. 96)

Dean Henry Alford was also quite definite on this subject: "The counsel and foreknowledge of God are not to be joined . . . as if they were the agents–the connexion in the original is that of accordance and appointment, not agency. . . . The counsel and foreknowledge of God are not the same; the former designates His eternal plan, by which He has arranged all things (hence the determinate counsel)–the latter, the omniscience, by which every part of this plan is foreseen and unforgotten by Him." (*New Testament for English Readers,* Vol. I, Part II, p. 661)

Again, on the word *foreknowledge,* W. E. Vine said: "The foreknowledge of God is the basis of His foreordaining counsels. . . . Foreknowledge is one aspect of omniscience. . . . God's foreknowledge involves His electing grace, but this does not preclude human will. He foreknows the exercise of faith which brings salvation." (*Expository Dictionary of New Testament Words,* Vol. II, p. 119)

The great continental scholar Godet has some pointed words on the subject and while extended, they are so pertinent, also showing how this is related to predestination, that we give the highlights: "The decree of predestination is founded on the act of foreknowledge. What does St. Paul understand by this last word? Some have given to the word *foreknow* the meaning of elect, choose, destine, beforehand (Calvin, etc.). Not only is this meaning arbitrary, as being without example in the New Testament, and as even in profane Greek the word *to know* has the meaning of deciding only when it applies to a thing, as when we say: to judge of a case, and never when applied to a person; but what is still more decidedly opposed to this meaning is what follows: *He did also predestinate*; for in that case the two verbs would be identical in meaning, and could not be connected by the particle of gradation, *also,* especially in view of [Romans 8] verse 30, where the successive degrees of divine action are strictly distinguished and graduated. . . . There is not a passage in the New Testament where the word *know* does not above all contain the notion of *knowledge* properly so called. The same is the case with the word *foreknow*. . . . In what respect did God thus foreknow them? . . . There is but one answer: foreknown as sure to fulfill the condition of salvation, viz., faith; so: foreknown as His by faith. Such is the meaning to which a host of commentators have been led, St. Augustine himself in early times, then the Lutheran expositors. . . . It is not the act of seeing or knowing which creates this object; it is this object, on the contrary, which determines the act of knowing or seeing. And the same is the case with divine prevision or foreknowledge. . . . Therefore it is the believer's faith, as a future fact, but in His sight already existing, which determines His foreknowledge. This faith does not exist because God sees it; He sees it, on the contrary, because it will come into being at a given moment, in time. . . . Reuss is certainly mistaken, therefore, in saying of these two verbs that substantially they denote 'one and the same act.' The object of the decree is not faith at all, as if God had said: As for thee, thou shalt believe; as for thee, thou shalt not believe. The object of predestination is glory: 'I see thee believing. . . . I will therefore that thou be glorified like My Son.' Such is the meaning of the decree. The predestination of which Paul speaks is not a predestination to faith, but a predestination to glory, founded on the prevision of faith. . . . What the decree of predestination embraces is the realization of the image of the Son in all foreknown believers." (F. Godet, *Commentary on St. Paul's Epistle to the Romans, Vol. II, pp. 108-110)*

Then, in a later section of the same commentary, Godet

has some further remarks, along with which he presents an interesting illustration of God's foreknowledge and how it fits into His larger plan: "A multitude of expositors . . . have endeavored to find a formula whereby to combine the action of man's moral freedom with the divine predestination. . . . We are convinced that it is only in this way that the true thought of the apostle can be explained. . . . As to the speculative question of the relation between God's eternal plan and the freedom of human determinations, it seems to me probable that Paul resolved it, so far as he was himself concerned, by means of the fact affirmed by him, of *divine foreknowledge.* He himself puts us on this way [Romans] 8:29-30, by making foreknowledge the basis of predestination. As a general, who is in full acquaintance with the plans of campaign adopted by the opposing general, would organize his own in keeping with this certain prevision, and would find means of turning all the marches and countermarches of his adversary to the success of his designs; so God, after fixing the supreme end, employs the free human actions, which He contemplates from the depths of His eternity, as factors to which He assigns a part, and which He makes so many means in the realization of His eternal design." (*Ibid.,* pp. 189,191)

Dr. H. G. Thiessen viewed things similarly. On election he said: "It is based on the foreknowledge of God and not on caprice or arbitrary will. Foreknowledge is not of itself causative, although there are some things which God foreknows simply because He expects efficaciously to bring them about. There are other things which He foreknows because He has purposed to permit them to come; and still other things which He foreknows because He foresees what men will do without causing them to do them. If He cannot foreknow the latter, then He cannot have foreknown that sin would come before it was committed. . . . God foreknew what men would do in response to His common grace; and He elected those whom He foresaw would respond positively. . . . He chose those whom He foreknew would accept Christ.

The Scriptures definitely base God's election on His foreknowledge: 'Whom He foreknew He also foreordained . . . and whom He foreordained, them He also called' (Romans 8:29-30); 'to the . . . elect according to the foreknowledge of God the Father' (1 Peter 1:1-2). [American Standard Version, 1901] Although we are nowhere told what it is in the foreknowledge of God that determines His choice, the repeated teaching of Scripture that man is responsible for accepting or rejecting salvation necessitates our postulating that it is man's reaction to the revelation God has made of Himself that is the basis of His election. . . . In His foreknowledge He perceives what each one will do with this restored ability, and elects men to salvation in harmony with His knowledge of their choice of Him. There is no merit in this transaction. . . . Election is based on foreknowledge. This is in accord with Scripture. To say that God foreknew all things because He had arbitrarily determined all things, is to ignore the distinction between God's efficient and His permissive decrees." (*Lectures in Systematic Theology,* pp. 157, 344-345)

E. H. Johnson, in one of the old standard Baptist works on theology, said: "Predestination to eternal life is plainly conditioned upon the foreknowledge of God. . . . What ever else 'foreknow' may mean, it means foreknow."

Then, while admitting that anti-Calvinists need not insist that foreseen faith is the condition of election, he said: "The Calvinist need not deny that foreseen faith can be the condition of election. His only evangelical interest is to avoid the doctrine that men can be saved by works. But freedom of grace is assured even though faith be a condition of election. . . . If, without disparagement to grace, faith can be the condition of justification, why might it not be the condition of election? That it is such the Bible nowhere states nor is there any way of knowing; but, inasmuch as salvation is received as a gift only on condition of faith exercised, it is in purpose a gift, even if only on condition of faith foreseen. Election is not the less sovereign if conditioned upon foreknowledge of faith. Foreknowing what His creatures would do, God decreed their destiny. . . ." (*An Outline of Systematic Theology,* second edition, Johnson and Weston, pp. 247,250-251)

Dr. Leander S. Keyser, the afore-mentioned writer and professor of theology, not only declared himself, but showed the cogent reasons for this position: "Even if God did, by virtue of His foreknowledge, elect believers unto salvation, in view of their faith, it would not destroy the heavenly doctrine of *sola gratia* (solely by grace), because faith simply accepts the gratuity from the hands of the God of love and mercy. In view of the fact, therefore, that justification by faith connotes salvation by grace alone, we would not deem it unworthy of the wise and holy God to predestine unto eternal life those who He foresaw from eternity would believe on the Redeemer whom He foreordained from eternity to save them. . . . If He foreordained that they should be saved through faith in Christ (as He did), surely it would not be out of accord with His whole wonderful and gracious scheme, if He should have foreordained that those who He foresaw would exercise such faith should be chosen and kept unto life. . . . Surely if God honors faith so much as to make it the vehicle of justification in time, it would not derogate from His honor for Him to have taken it into consideration in the counsels of eternity. . . . It is plain that God must have foreordained the whole plan of redemption in view of sin. Then why might He not predetermine salvation in view of faith? And if foreordination in view of sin would not dishonor Him, why would foreordination in view of faith dishonor Him? All the more so, since sin is something entirely obnoxious to Him and contrary to His will, while faith is a holy principle. . . . If in time He has revealed persevering faith to be the condition of salvation, He must have foreordained it to be so from eternity. Surely, then, for those who He foreknew would comply with His plainly announced condition, He would make His predetermination effective. Thus the election must have been 'in view of faith.' And remember, 'it is by faith that it might be by grace.' " (*Election and Conversion*, pp. 28-29,113)

Some have suggested that foreknowledge merely conveys the idea that God foreknew the saved because He had elected them to salvation, and they read that thought into Romans 8:29, "whom He foreknew, He also foreordained" (R. V). To this, Dr. Keyser responds: "If you read it thus: 'For whom He foreknew that He would foreordain, them He foreordained . . .' [it] would be tantamount to saying: 'Whom He foreordained them He foreordained'; and that would make Paul a vapid writer. If Paul meant by 'foreknew' 'foreordained,' why did he not use the right word?" (*Ibid.*, p. 140)

Dr. Nathan E. Wood, of the old Newton Theological Institution, showed the human involvement in election and then its theological relations: "The election of men is not based on a decree of sovereignty regardless of any qualities in the man, but it takes account of the habit of openness to moral appeal, which God sees in the man and which the man has himself fostered. 'Whom He foresees, He foreordains.' . . . If it is meant that there is a difference in goodness or merit in men which becomes the ground of an effectual call, it cannot be admitted. It is true that there are differences in goodness in men, but it is not the ground of the effectual call. If it is meant that there are differences in the habit of open-mindedness toward moral truth, it may be true that differences in disposition may be the opportunity, on the human side, for an effectual call." (*The Person and Work of Jesus Christ, An Exposition of Christian Doctrine*, pp. 133-134,140-141)

Along with this, Dr. Wood took up the ground of election and gave four possible views. The first three he rejected, the third of which is: "God chooses men to salvation for reasons which are known only to Himself. He has not chosen to reveal them. He acts out of His own sovereign good pleasure. . . . This is the usual Augustinian or Calvinistic view. It somehow leaves the impression in the human mind that God's choice is arbitrary. . . . Much may be urged against this third view. . . . The objection to this view is that it conceives a freedom for God which is greater than is necessary for electing men, and a freedom for man which is less than is necessary for responsibility for sin." (*Ibid.*, pp.129-130)

Dr. Wood found the answer (in the fourth view) in the moral nature of man: "Man's distinction among created things is that he has a moral nature. Whatever loss or ruin has been wrought by sin in the moral nature, the remainders of that nature, which are essential to moral responsibility, still persist. . . . It is possible then, that God chooses some men to salvation because He foresees or foreknows that there is something in the character of their will which will respond to appeals made by Him. . . . God foresees that some wills are reachable, or get-at-able by the proper presentation of motives. They have acquired a habit of candor in the consideration of moral questions." (*Ibid.*, pp. 130-131)

Dr. Wood then presented "The Scripture representations concerning the attitudes of closedness or openness of mind toward Christ and His message." He listed Acts 17:11; Matthew 10:14-15; Luke 10:11; Matthew 12:41-42; Luke 11:32; Matthew 22:5; 13:19-23; Mark 4:15-20; Matthew 11:21; 7:25-27; John 5:24; 6:40; Matthew 12:30; John 3:19; 5:40; briefly characterizing these passages.

Dr. Wood finally said, "The view herein set forth may be called moderately Calvinistic." (*Ibid.*, p. 137)

Dr. George P. Pardington, in a widely-used book on doctrine, said: "Redemptive election may be defined as God's determination from eternity to save certain individuals, apart from any merit of their own, on the ground of their foreseen faith. . . . The Greek word rendered 'foreknow' implies prescience of character." (*Outline Studies in Christian Doctrine*, pp. 313-314)

Even Dr. William Evans in his well-known book on doctrine wrote: "We must not confound the foreknowledge of God with His foreordination. The two things are, in a sense, distinct. The fact that God foreknows a thing makes that thing certain but not necessary. His foreordination is based upon His foreknowledge." (*The Great Doctrines of the Bible*, p. 31)

Dr. A. J. Wall presented a pointed illustration: "Just because God knew that men would 'make his calling and election sure' (2 Peter 1:10) does not mean that He prefixed the election. A simple illustration will explain what this Scripture means. Two men were watching a television program. One of the two men had seen the program before. Therefore this man knew what was going to happen all the way to the end, but he did not prefix it so that it would happen. He foresaw what was going to happen, but he did not prefix it and therefore was not responsible for what happened in the picture. God from the beginning saw the end.... Does this mean that God elected every murder, every act of drunkenness, every act of adultery, every person to be saved, or every person not to believe because He saw the end from the beginning? Can one blame God with all the crime in the universe, all the bloodshed, all immorality, just because He foresaw that they would take place?" (*The Truth About Election*, pp. 7-8)

Having noted the theological and exegetical groundwork of this position, we may note how some have briefly declared themselves on it.

Dr. Harry Ironside, as previously cited, said, "Scripture plainly teaches election based upon God's foreknowledge." (*What's The Answer*, p. 54)

In *What Baptists Believe*, H. H. Hobbs said: "The Bible teaches that God does foreknow man's choices.... Foreknowledge is also related to election (1 Peter 1:2). This refers to the election of individuals only in the sense that God foreknew who would receive or reject His provision for sin (cf. Romans 8:29). But even God's foreknowledge leaves man free and responsible in his choice.... An omniscient God knew beforehand who would reject or accept His salvation. But His foreknowledge does not make Him responsible for man's choice." (pp. 25-26,107)

On some of the same Scripture references, F. B. Meyer commented: " 'According to the foreknowledge of God the Father.' From all eternity He knew those who would accept the overtures of mercy. Shall we say that He foresaw the certain affinity between the elect One and those who would cleave to Him by faith?" (*Tried By Fire,* p. 13)

Similarly, Dr. Meyer said (on Romans 9), "There is no caprice with God. . . . Any apparent change in His dealings is determined by *our* attitude toward Him." (*Through The Bible Day by Day,* Vol. VI, p. 90)

Dr. G. Campbell Morgan said: " 'Foreordained to be conformed to the image of His Son.' God's election of certain persons to constitute His Church is not capricious, but has regard to character. He foreordained those whom He foreknew, in order that they might be conformed to the image of His Son." (*God's Methods With Man,* p. 174)

Again, Dr. Morgan wrote: "The purpose of election was character, and its principle was the mercy and compassion of God. God exercises that mercy toward those who believe. . . . The Gentiles are chosen to become a people of God, because they attain righteousness by faith, while Israel failed as a nation, through seeking to establish righteousness apart from faith. Thus the choice of God is of such as believe. The test is the Son of His love." (*The Analyzed Bible,*"Introduction, Matthew to Revelation," p. 103)

Dr. E. Schuyler English said: "In His foreknowledge, though He so loved the world that *whosoever* believeth in Christ shall not perish, but have everlasting life, He knew who would believe and receive His Son, and who would reject Him. He foreknew, and in His foreknowledge He chose some out of the world, and them He did predestinate to become conformed to the image of His Son, and be to the praise of His glory." (*The Life and Letters of Saint Peter,* p. 156)

Even Dr. R. A. Torrey declared: "The actions of Judas and the rest were taken into God's plan, and thus made a part of it. But it does not mean that these men were not perfectly free in their choice. They did not do as they did because God knew that they would do so, but the fact that they would do so was the basis upon which God knew it. Foreknowledge no more determines a man's actions than afterknowledge.

Knowledge is determined by the fact, not the fact by the knowledge. . . . God knows from all eternity what each man will do, whether he will yield to the Spirit and accept Christ, or whether he will resist the Spirit and refuse Christ. Those who will receive Him are ordained to eternal life. If any are lost it is simply because they will not come to Christ and thus obtain life (John 5:40). Whosoever will may come (Revelation 22:17), and all who do come will be received (John 6:37)." (*Practical and Perplexing Questions Answered,* p. 61)

More recently, Dr. J. Sidlow Baxter said: "It is in the light of His perfect foreknowledge that He preadapts and prearranges and predetermines. Thus, while He never leaves His ultimate purposes at the mercy of human uncertainty, in the outworking of things to the predetermined end He recognizes the free will of man all through, and prearranges according to His foreknowledge of what man will do." (*Explore the Book,* Vol. VI, pp. 47-48)

Dr. Lehman Strauss is on record saying, "God's foreknowledge . . . does not in any wise rule out the Biblical truth of free agency in man. . . . In the matter of an individual's acceptance or rejection of Jesus Christ as Saviour, it is only fair to add that God knows what that individual will do." (*The Atonement of Christ,* p. 13)

Finally, we may conclude this section with a statement by William E. Gladstone, said by some to be the greatest mind produced by the Anglo-Saxon nation. In a footnote in his edition of Butler's *Analogy* he wrote: "Some hold that 'necessity' is admissible and just, in the sense of foreknowledge. . . . But, surely as vision is a thing totally separate from causation, so is prevision: and it is a confusion of ideas to mix certainty with necessity." (p. 131)

CHAPTER 7

SOME IMPLICATIONS OF THE SUBJECT AND POSSIBLE ATTITUDES

Having covered some major aspects of the subject, and having seen what a wide range of scholars have set forth thereon, before leaving our theme it may be well to consider some of its possible implications, and note how the viewpoint held may influence one's outlook.

To start with, it is sometimes asserted, as though it explained everything, that we must remember that the means are preordained as well as the end or the final outcome.

If by this it is meant merely that God has appointed that through the proclamation of the gospel men are to be saved, we readily agree. Indeed, "it pleased God by the foolishness of preaching to save them that believe" (1 Corinthians 1:21). The place of the Holy Spirit, the printed Word, etc., are also recognized.

However, it is also possible to carry it further. It could be made to include the thought that God has decreed that the elect will, due to the very fact that they are elect, be prompted to exercise the necessary saving faith, and exercise it in response to certain means, such as preaching, all of which have also been predetermined.

That being the case, the elect will be saved by the ordained means which are as sure as their election. All, apparently, is controlled by God, both the agency and the end. Those who preach do it, in the last analysis, only because it is decreed that they shall do so. Those who believe, likewise believe simply because it was so decreed. Man, it would seem, still exercises no part for which he is really responsible.

It would be natural to ask, then, why should not the unsaved sit back in indifference, knowing that if it is decreed that he will believe, he will be impelled to believe, and that, in the decreed time and manner, and only in such?

It is easy to say, as is often done, that the doctrine of election is not for the unsaved. But can we keep people in general from knowing what we believe is the way in which God operates? Holding back on something does not change the picture. It doesn't seem fair to imply that one has a free chance, and then when the results are in, tell him that it was all settled beforehand.

The principle being established that the means are decreed as well as the end, may not the principle be carried over, perhaps unconsciously, into the area of Christian activity? To illustrate, it would appear to indicate for the would-be Christian worker, that not only is it preordained which particular souls out there in the world around him are going to be saved, but also by just what instrumentality or means they are going to be brought into that state. That being the case, the reasoning would be, why should one concern himself in the matter of going out after the lost, for, if any particular individual is going to be saved, he will certainly be saved irrespective of what one of us may or may not do about it. And if the means is fully ordained, I am, for example, either that ordained means or I am not. If I am, I will be impelled to go after that lost soul, come what may, and if I am not the ordained means, it will do me no good to go out after the lost anyway, for in spite of all my earnest desire, nothing will come of it. The same would apply equally to the agency of sowing the seed as well as drawing the net.

However, the scriptural exhortations for the child of God to show compassion upon the lost, to warn them of their peril, and to plead with them to come to the Saviour, appear to leave little room for such a viewpoint.

At this juncture it is commonly asserted that we are still

under full responsibility to preach the gospel to all, because God has commanded us to do so, and also because we do not know who, among those to whom we preach, are elected to be saved and who are not. Some may feel that these considerations are sufficient to assure the continuance of proper Christian witness, and to give us an area in which to occupy ourselves.

But in spite of these repeated assertions, it seems that the above philosophy is bound to soften the sense of obligation in going out after the lost. Even though we do not know who the elect are, only those who are elect will respond to preaching or to personal work; and if elect, it appears that they are sure to respond regardless of urgent appeal or no such appeal. This is certainly contrary to the spirit of challenges commonly put before believers to the effect that much hinges upon the way they endeavor to be living witnesses to the saving grace that is in Christ.

In fact, there has been a deploring of a certain kind of preaching in which the truth was propounded in a cold, matter-of-fact way, and the "invitation" presented in a manner which seemed to say: there it is, take it or leave it; if you are among the elect, you will respond, if you are not, you will not respond anyway. No wonder missionary leaders are deeply concerned by the fact that Wesleyan and Pentecostal groups in Latin America are increasing at an astonishingly greater rate than our more staid and conventional groups. They at least (in spite of points on which we cannot concur with them), go out after their fellow men as if each and every one could and should respond to the gospel. It has been observed that they show a concern and a tenderness and a sense of urgency lacking in those who are assured that all is already fixed and determined in the plan of God.

Dr. Henry C. Thiessen recognized the problem here and stated the case in these words: "Christ sent His disciples into all the world, and He instructed them to preach the gospel to every creature. If, then, election means that all those whom God has arbitrarily chosen will certainly get to Heaven, and that all those whom He has not chosen will certainly not get there, no matter how faithfully and frequently the gospel may be preached to them, then why be greatly agitated about it? True, we have the command to take the gospel into all the world; but if only some are thus 'elected,' why be greatly disturbed about it?" (*Lectures in Systematic Theology,* p.347)

With the all-is-settled view suggested, men will naturally be inclined to reason, consciously or unconsciously—unconsciously, no doubt, for most—that irrespective of what is done, God's will is being fulfilled and that all will come out as it should anyway. The tendency then is to settle down thinking duty is being done; why further exert or inconvenience oneself?

Revival too, among careless and shallow Christians, it may be reasoned, will come if it is in the plan of God for them; and if either the Christian's prayers or his efforts are to be the means to such an end, he will be irresistibly impelled to expend the time and energy necessary just to the extent that it has been preordained. Why then, should anyone weep over either lost souls or cold and faithless people of God? Why, in sorrow of heart, plead with those in need as if anything were up to them?

In the comprehensive work, *Baptist Doctrines,* from which quotation has already been made, we find the writer on this general subject, Dr. Richard Fuller, pointedly declared himself: "Some theologians profess to . . . undertake to reconcile the difficulties of our subject by this solution: that God, who appoints the end, appoints also the means. . . . But it elucidates nothing, it only removes the difficulty one step farther. The advocates of this thesis do not belong to a third class, they are Necessarians, and ascribe all events to God's decrees as rigorously as if no agent had been employed. . . . Nothing is gained by it. The unthinking may be thus satisfied; but it is an old axiom, that he who performs an act by another, performs it himself. In human affairs God never acts immediately, except when working miracles; He uses instruments and agents. These, of course, are chosen by Him; and if they are necessitated by His decrees—as is supposed in the case before us—the introduction of one or many agencies produces no modification in the system, which is that of mechanical force and stern compulsion. . . . A preacher may think that he has triumphed, when he thus disposes of an objection; but he deceives himself . . . he has not fairly met the difficulty; he has only shifted it a little out of sight.

"In the recital from which our text is taken [Acts 27], Paul announced, by express revelation from Heaven, that not a soul on board the ship should perish. Yet when the seamen were about to leave in the boats, he as confidently declared that unless they remained in the vessel the passengers could not be saved. According to the intermediate system, the apostle was very inconsistent in this last admonition; since he must have seen clearly that if God had predetermined the salvation of all, He had also indefeasibly adjusted the means, and that His decree could no more be frustrated by the treachery of mariners than by the wind and the waves." (pp. 494-495)

In the chapter in Acts just cited others have seen the same truth. A writer in *The Pulpit Commentary* declared: "If God had given Paul 'all them that sailed with him,' and this so certainly that the apostle could say without qualification, 'there shall be no loss of any man's life' (verse 22), how could the desertion of the shipmen (verse 31) have imperiled the safety of the passengers so that Paul exclaimed, 'Except these abide,' etc.? The answer to the question is found in the truth that *God's promises to His children are always conditional on their obedience to His will.* So truly is this the case, and so practically, that it is not only possible we may bring about the nonfulfillment of the divine promises, but certain that we shall do so, if we do not comply with the conditions which are expressed or understood. We may find: I. Historical illustrations of this principle. 1. Genesis 1:26-31 and 6:5-7. 2. Exodus 3:7-8 and Numbers 14:28-34. 3. 2 Samuel 7:12-16 and 1 Kings 11:11-13 with 1 Kings 12:16. II. Individual illustrations of it. . . . We know that it is the will of God that all who hear the gospel should be saved by it (1 Timothy 2:4; 2 Peter 3:9; Ezekiel 33:11). But we also know that those will never enter the kingdom who will not repent and believe (John 3:36; 5:40; Acts 13:46)." (Clarkson in "The Acts of the Apostles," Vol. II, p. 307)

Rackham, in his commentary on Acts, somewhat similarly said: "Knowing that the fulfillment of the divine promises is not absolute but conditioned, he prayed. . . . More than for himself he was anxious for the safety of his fellow shipmates. . . . He exhorts them to take heart and be like men: and this because effort will be required on their part. There are conditions on which the fulfillment of the divine promise depends: and God requires on man's part co-operation or correspondence to His will. Of such necessary conditions or essential means we shall find three instances. . . . The fulfillment of the divine will, however, depended upon the proper co-operation of man's part. . . . The soldiers showed their faith in St. Paul by cutting the ropes and sacrificing the boat; and by so doing they may have saved the lives of the sailors in spite of themselves. A second condition needful for their safety was to take some food. The work of getting to shore [the third condition] would require all their strength and nerve. . . ." *(The Acts of the Apostles,* pp. 486-487,489)

In *The Expositor's Bible,* G. T. Stokes put it this way: "The will of God was revealed to him that he had been given all the souls that sailed with him. . . . But the knowledge of God's purposes did not cause his exertions to relax. He knew that God's promises are conditional upon man's exertions, and therefore he urged his companions to be fellow-workers with God in the matter of their own salvation from impending death." (Vol. II, p. 364)

Brief concurring statements come from two well-known Baptists from across the sea. Dr. W. Graham Scroggie said: "Most of the divine promises can be fulfilled only if and when human conditions are co-operative. Means and end must harmonize (Acts 27:24,31). Paul said: 'Unless . . . you cannot be saved.' " (*The Unfolding Drama of Redemption,* Vol. II, p. 471)

Alexander Maclaren observed on this passage: "The lesson often drawn from his words is rightly drawn. They imply the necessity of men's action in order to carry out God's purposes." (*Expositions of Holy Scripture,* "Acts of the Apostles," II, p. 365)

There is, then, a real sense in which there is need for a greater recognition of the responsibility resting upon man. Illustrating the need for a deep sense of concern and the importance of pressing on with the claims of the gospel, are the words of one of America's notable Baptist preachers. Dr. George C. Lorimer was the celebrated pastor of Tremont Temple, Boston, and was recognized as an outstanding pulpit orator, a keen observer, and the author of a number of widely-read works. He commented on C. H. Spurgeon's example and on the importance of avoiding a lifeless pulpit ministry. In his biographical memoir of Spurgeon he said: "It ought to be known and remembered that the religious life of England shriveled and almost died beneath the style of preaching that had for its chief ornament and exponent the famous Dr. South [a pronounced Calvinist]. . . . If history, therefore, teaches anything, it teaches that a fixed and settled purpose to arouse men to a sense of their sins, and to deliver them from indifference to the claims of God, to move their consciences and change their life, is indispensable to the sacred calling, if that calling is to be redeemed from the contumacious sneers of the world, and to be in any true sense a service of helpfulness to the race. . . .

"John Wesley was renowned in the Saviour's vineyard, and yet sympathized but little with Calvin's harsher dogmas. Others also have been honored in extending the triumphs of the King of kings who have firmly rejected these views; and in my opinion it is questionable whether the success of the preachers who espouse them is not proportionate to their silence regarding them rather than to their proclamation." (*Charles Haddon Spurgeon,* pp. 80-82)

PART 2

SCRIPTURES CALLING FOR SPECIAL ATTENTION

In view of all that has gone before, some may wonder what, then, is to be done with certain passages of Scripture which might be assumed to furnish grounds for a different viewpoint than that indicated in the foregoing pages.

A number of such passages have already come into view, some in an incidental way. The careful reader will already have seen the point of many of these. But for the sake of more specific comment, several of these passages should be considered.

Not every single text which, on occasion, may have seemed to present a difficulty in this connection is included, but in considering some of the most puzzling ones it may be seen how others could similarly be brought into focus.

We acknowledge that in a number of instances other interpretations than those herein set forth have been presented. Here we merely point out that the viewpoints to which we call attention are not only possible, but that recognized authorities hold to them, and believe that they have reason for so doing.

In considering some of these problem texts, one thing of help may be merely to note some other verses, often right in the context, which present another phase of things. It may be objected that these other verses do not of themselves change the meaning of the main text under consideration. However, the point is that these additional verses should be considered as well as the problem text, which frequently has not been the case. Too commonly only one aspect of the subject has been looked at and any complementary side wholly ignored. Our conviction is that one truth is commonly balanced by another truth set forth. That another side may be found, and that frequently not far away, of itself shows that the one needs the other in order to get the complete picture.

It will perhaps come as a surprise to some readers to see how certain familiar verses of Scripture could and have been given a connotation which ordinarily would not have been associated with them. But these verses may not necessarily demand the rigid system which, on occasion, has been read into them. A forthright facing of them is the best way to dispose of these problems.

Matthew 20:16b—"For many be called, but few chosen."

Matthew 22:14—"For many are called, but few are chosen."

These phrases at first seem puzzling, but can be rendered in simple terms. H. A. Ironside explained it: "When our Lord tells us that 'many are called, but few are chosen,' He means that while the call goes out to the multitude, only those are chosen who definitely accept Christ." (*What's the Answer?* p. 52)

A. T. Robertson gave a similar brief explanation: "The people of Palestine had been invited by Jesus, but few had responded." (*Commentary on the Gospel According to Matthew,* p. 229)

So also, William L. Pettingill said: "For many are called—'invited' here—but few chosen. Those are 'chosen' who put on the wedding garment provided by the King." (*Simple Studies in Matthew,* p. 277)

Jamieson, Fausset, and Brown's commentary says on this,

'What divines call effectual calling . . . cannot be the meaning of it here; the 'called' being emphatically distinguished from the 'chosen.' It can only mean here the 'invited.' " (On Matthew 20:16)

The *Pulpit Commentary* on the same text says: "It would seem that Christ takes occasion from the particular case in the parable to make a general statement, that not all who are called would receive reward, because many would not answer the call, or would nullify it by their conduct; not, as Theophylact says, that salvation is limited, but men's efforts to obtain it are feeble or negative." ("Matthew," Vol. II, p. 278)

Some apply the words to final rewards for faithfulness, others apply them to the kind of response made to the preaching of the gospel. Dr. Arno C. Gaebelein took the words in the twentieth chapter in the first sense, the statement in the twenty-second chapter in the latter sense. He said on the first: " 'Many are called, but few are chosen ones,' which has nothing to do with salvation, but is in connection with rewards." (*The Gospel of Matthew,* Vol. II, p. 113) On the second he said: "The many which are called are all those who heard the call and made an outward profession, without having accepted the Lord Jesus Christ. . . . In a general way He teaches this as a warning that though His invitation goes forth and many hear, yet not all will be chosen and that simply because they refuse to accept the gift of God." (pp. 144-145)

Oliver B. Greene in a radio sermon said: "What does this verse mean anyway? 'For many are called, but few are chosen.' In this chapter [22] the Lord Jesus gives the parable of the marriage feast. Those who were invited refused to attend. So the Lord said to the servants, 'Go . . . into the highways, and as many as ye shall find, bid to the feast.' The servants did as they were commanded and the wedding was furnished with guests. Many were invited who did not attend —for one reason or another they did not come. . . . They refused to come. Then the invitation was sent to all. Many were invited, but few were chosen–few came upon the strength of the invitation. In this marvelous day of grace tens of thousands are hearing the gospel, and by hearing the gospel they are invited to attend the marriage supper of the Lamb; but few are accepting the invitation. Many are being called through the gospel message–the Word calls, but they refuse to answer the call. Those who answer the call are chosen to sit at the marriage supper in the sky (Revelation 19:7-10)." (*Predestination,* pp. 21-22)

Finally, in a message on Matthew 22:1-14, Alexander Maclaren concluded by saying: "They who do not choose to receive the invitation, or to put on the wedding garment, do, in different ways, show that they are not 'chosen' though 'called.' The lesson is not of interminable and insoluble questionings about God's secrets, but of earnest heed to His gracious call, and earnest, believing effort to make the fair garment our very own, 'If so be that being clothed we shall not be found naked.'" (*Expositions of Holy Scripture,* Matthew XVIII ff., p. 135)

John 6:44–"No man can come to Me, except the Father which hath sent Me draw him."

Taken in the light of the context this verse is not such a problem as it might seem. The very next verse (45) says, "It is written in the prophets, And they shall be all taught of God." The *all* must not be overlooked. As some have said, the Father is willing to draw all who are willing to be drawn. In verse 51 Jesus said, "I am the living bread. . . . If any man eat of this bread, he shall live for ever." If *any* man. And this later verse concludes, "My flesh, which I will give for the life of *the world.*"

Verse 44 is preceded by verse 40, the last words in each of which are identical. Verse 40 says, "This is the will of Him that sent Me, that every one which seeth the Son, and believeth on Him, may have everlasting life. . . ." So, seeing and believing precedes the statement of the drawing. Similarly, verse 37, "All that the Father giveth Me shall come to Me," is preceded by verse 35, "he that cometh to Me shall never hunger; and he that believeth on Me shall never thirst."

Beside the immediate context, it is interesting to see significant statements in both the chapter before this one and in the chapter following. In chapter 5:40 Jesus revealed the responsible part which man plays, in the words, "And ye will not come to Me, that ye might have life." The indication is that they could come, but the fault was squarely on them, "ye will not." Then in the seventh chapter, verse 17, Jesus said, "If any man will do His will, he shall know of the doctrine," which shows that it is up to the individual, "if *any* man. . . ."

As to the being drawn, in 6:44, we need only to turn to chapter 12 to see its fuller development. In 12:32 Jesus said, "And I, if I be lifted up from the earth, will draw *all* men unto Me."

On this verse in chapter 12, F. Godet said: "Some limit the *all* to the elect; others give it this sense: men of every nation. . . . But *to draw* does not necessarily denote an effectual drawing. This word may refer only to the preaching of the cross throughout the whole world and the action of the Holy Spirit which accompanies it. This heavenly drawing is not irresistible." (*Commentary on the Gospel of John,* Vol. II, p. 228)

A baptist preacher and teacher, Dr. A. J. Wall, said: "The same word for 'draw' is used in John 12:32 that is used in John 6:44. No man can come without being drawn, and Jesus said, 'I will draw *all men* unto Me'; therefore all men have an equal chance to be saved. No one will be lost because he has not been drawn to Christ, but many will be lost who fail to believe and to yield to the drawing of Christ." (*The Truth About Election,* p. 20)

Another Baptist pastor and writer, Carey L. Daniel, said on this: "It is our belief that God the Father draws all men who hear the gospel preached in the power of the Spirit. This is not to say, of course, that they all yield to this magnetism. There be some who falsely interpret the word 'draw' as 'drag' or 'force,' and who thereby conclude that there are certain people who could not go to hell even if they wanted to and others that could not go to Heaven if they wanted to." (*The Bible's Seeming Contradictions,* pp. 45-46)

Even D. L. Moody, after quoting John 6:44, said: "Well, I say Christ *is* drawing men. 'I, if I be lifted up . . . will draw all men unto Me.' He is drawing men, but they will not come. God was in Christ reconciling the world unto Himself, and drawing men unto Him. That drawing is going on now, but many a heart is fighting against the strivings of the Spirit. God is drawing men heavenward, and the devil is drawing them hellward." (*Select Sermons,* p. 112)

Scholars well-acquainted with the original language give warrant for such views, as for example, Dean Alford, who said on John 6:44: "That this 'drawing' is not irresistible grace, is confessed even by Augustine himself, the great upholder of the doctrines of grace. 'If a man . . . comes unwillingly, he does not believe; if he does not believe, he does not come. For we do not run to Christ on our feet, but by faith; not with the movement of the body, but with the free will of the heart.'. . . The Greek expositors take the view which I have adopted above. . . . This *drawing* now is being exerted on all the world—in accordance with the Lord's prophecy (12:32) and His command (Matthew 28:19-20)." (*New Testament for English Readers,* "John," p. 521)

Similarly, Bishop Wordsworth declared: "God is ready to draw every man, for He says, It is written in the Prophets, they *shall all be* taught of God (Isaiah 54:13). . . . This saying does not deny our free will, which is the error of the Manichaeans, but proves our need for divine grace. . . . We have a Teacher who is willing to give His blessing to all (verse

45), and pours out His heavenly teaching upon all. God draws all who are willing to be drawn." *(The New Testament in the Original Greek, with Notes and Introductions,* Gospels, p.299)

The scholarly Timothy Dwight, president of Yale and translator of Godet's work on John, said in that volume in his own note on this text: "The general thought of this passage is similar to that of the verses which immediately precede—the nonreceptivity of the unsusceptible soul, and the life which the susceptible soul receives through Christ. . . . The whole development of thought in this discourse, which bears upon the inner life of the soul, seems to show clearly that, in such verses as 44 and 37, the question is not of God's electing purpose, but of the inward susceptibility to divine influence. And the same is true of other similar passages in this Gospel." (Vol. II, p.463)

Finally, G. Campbell Morgan said, following verse 44 by verse 45: "You cannot come to Me, said Jesus, except you are drawn; but that is no excuse for your ignorance, because God is drawing you; 'They shall all be taught of God.' " *(The Gospel According to John,* p. 115)

John 10:26—"But ye believe not, because ye are not of My sheep."

This statement is similar to those seen in the sixth chapter of John, and similar considerations apply to it.

In the verse immediately preceding, Jesus said, "I told you, and ye believed not." So their opportunity and their rejection of it in unbelief preceded this declaration.

A bit before that, in the same chapter, Jesus proclaimed, "I am the door: by Me if any man enter in, he shall be saved" (verse 9). The opportunity of being saved is open to "any man," and it is only after spurning it that any are said to be not of His sheep.

Alfred Plummer in *The Cambridge Bible* said: "The reference is to the general sense of the allegory of the sheepfold, especially verses 14-15. He and His sheep have most intimate knowledge of one another; therefore these Jews asking who He is prove that they are not His sheep. Compare 6:36, where there seems to be a similar reference to the general meaning of a previous discourse." (St. John, p. 220)

Milligan and Moulton, in the *International Revision Commentary,* said: "There is no reference to an essential or necessary state, to any 'decree' through the operation of which they were incapable of faith. They have not the character, the disposition, of His sheep; through this moral defect (for which they are themselves responsible, see chapter 3:19, etc.), they will not believe." (John, p. 241)

On this, Dr. A. C. Gaebelein said: "He had told them and they had not believed. All along, beginning with the fifth chapter in this Gospel, He had given this great witness about Himself. Furthermore, He had done the great works in the name of His Father, and all these works bore witness of Him. In spite of it all they were unbelievers and had rejected His own words and the witness of the Father. The Lord adds, 'But ye believe not, because ye are not of My sheep, as I said unto you.' That they were not His sheep was evidenced by their unbelief. The cause of their unbelief was not some kind of an election, which had marked them out before they ever were born, to be excluded from the flock the Shepherd came to gather; but it was their unbelief which was the cause of not becoming His sheep." (*The Gospel of John*, 187)

In the two-volume commentary on John by George Reith, which Dr. Wilbur Smith highly commends, we read on John 10:26: "The meaning would be simpler if the clauses were inverted. Ye are not of My sheep, because ye do not believe. The whole thought of the passage is based on a mutual understanding between Christ and His own. When He calls, they recognize His voice and follow Him. . . . Why were they not receptive? What answer can be made other than

Christ's own, Ye *will* not come to Me, that ye might have life (5:40)?" (*St. John's Gospel*, Vol. II, p. 46)

Godet, in his commentary on John, explained these verses in the light of the context: "If they *were willing* to believe, they had only to pronounce it themselves. Thus is His reply explained. . . . To His own testimony, if it does not appear to them sufficient, there is added, moreover, that of the Father. . . . If these testimonies failed with them, it is the result of their unbelief (verse 26). . . . The subject, *you*, placed at the beginning, signifies: It is not I, it is you, who are responsible for this result. And the following declaration: *You are not of My sheep*, shows them that the moral disposition is what is wanting to them that they may not recognize in Him the divine Shepherd." (Emphasis his. *Commentary on the Gospel of John*, Vol. II, p. 159)

John 12:39—"Therefore they could not believe."

This statement is in the same chapter as verse 32 already referred to, "I, if I be lifted up from the earth, will draw all men unto Me." The "all men" is comprehensive in its sweep.

The context should not be overlooked. Verses 35-36 appeal to the hearers to avail themselves of the light and to believe. And then following verse 39, in verse 46 we find "whosoever believeth," and in verse 47 "if any man hear."

On verse 39, J. C. Ryle said: "This . . . cannot of course mean that the Jews were unable to believe, although really desirous to do so, and were prevented by the prophecy of Isaiah. What then can it mean? The following paraphrase is offered. 'This was the cause why they could not believe: they were in that state of judicial blindness and hardness which Isaiah had described; they were justly given over to this state because of their many sins: and for this cause they had no power to believe.'. . . It precisely describes the moral inability of a thoroughly hardened and wicked man to believe. He is thoroughly under the mastery of a hardened and seared conscience, and has, as it were, lost the power of believing. . . . Even in our own English language the expression, 'could not,' is sometimes used in the sense of 'would not.' Thus the brethren of Joseph 'hated him, and could not speak peaceably unto him' (Genesis 37:4)." (*Expository Thoughts on St. John*, Vol. II, p. 415)

Quite similarly the *Pulpit Commentary* says: "That which in all the several quotations of this passage we learn from Isaiah's oracle is that the unforced and willful rejection of the Divine Word is visited by condign withdrawment of the faculty to receive even more accessible and apprehensible truth. This is the great law of divine operation in the nature of all moral beings. . . . They could not believe, because, on the principle involved in Isaiah's predictions, the divine government had fulfilled itself, had acted upon its universal law, and in consequence, they had thus fallen into the curse that belongs to a neglect of the divine. 'They could not believe.' Thus even now disinclination to God and to righteousness leads to moral incapacity. Sin is punished by its natural consequences: unbelief is punished by unsusceptibility to clearest evidence; prejudice by blindness; rejection of divine love by inability to see it at its best." (*The Pulpit Commentary*, "John," Vol. II, p. 146)

Godet on John drew the conclusion: "It is clear that, in the midst of this national judgment, every *individual* remained free to turn to God by repentance and to escape the general hardening. Verse 13 of Isaiah 6 and verse 42 of John 12 are proof of this. . . . The real cause of Jewish unbelief, foretold by God, is not the divine foreseeing. This cause is, in the last analysis, the moral state of the people themselves." (*Commentary on the Gospel of John*, Vol. II, p. 235)

G. Campbell Morgan said on this: "It must be remembered that God never hardens a man until the man has hardened his own heart. John has quoted freely from Isaiah.

. . . He confirmed their own decision. It is exactly the same in the story of Pharaoh. The Lord at last hardened Pharaoh's heart, but not till Pharaoh had hardened his own heart. . . . We are certainly not to understand by this summary of John that unbelief was the result of a divine action, preventing belief. God does not do that. He does ratify human decision. If in spite of all the signs, men refuse the evidence of the signs, there comes the hour when that choice is ratified by God, and they pass into the realm of blindness. That summarizes the whole of that mission of our Lord. . . . God ratified a decision and an attitude, to which men had come of their own choice." (*The Gospel According to John*, p. 223)

Showing how the truth here may become an actuality, Dr. Wm. E. Biederwolf said: "A man could not be penitent if he had committed the unpardonable sin. This is the meaning of John 12:39: 'Therefore they could not believe.' They had so repeatedly refused to believe, in the day when that power was still with them, that their faith faculty had become atrophied. . . . Now if you will imagine the history of these Jews you will discover the nature of the unpardonable sin. The opposition of these blaspheming Jews did not begin on the day He cured the unhappy demoniac and it did not end there. It began further back, at the very beginning of His ministry. Time and again evidence of His divinity flashed out before them, but they shut their eyes and would not see. . . . They hardened their hearts and said, 'He is not the Son of God.' . . . You may so set your will against God that your will becomes fixed, and when this is so, what was said of those Jews may be likewise said of you, 'Therefore they could not believe.'. . . Harden your heart long enough, refusing to use it for the purpose God gave it to you, and the time will come when your heart will have lost forever the capacity to feel and believe." (*Evangelistic Sermons, Doctrinal Series,* pp. 193,194-195,198-199)

John 15:16—"Ye have not chosen Me, but I have chosen you."

Problems arise here only when one stops in the middle of the verse. Read on, and when the whole statement is taken it will be seen to apply to service or labor performed in the Lord's vineyard: "that ye should go and bring forth fruit . . . fruit should remain."

Marvin R. Vincent said on this verse: "He has appointed them *that* they should bring forth fruit, and *that* they should obtain such answers to their prayers as would make them fruitful." (Emphasis his. *Word Studies in the New Testament,* Vol. II, p. 253)

Some take it as including Christian service in general; others, indeed, take it as applying almost exclusively to the apostles.

G. Campbell Morgan said on this text: "He was talking to the eleven, of course; but through them He was talking to all whom they represented. . . . I chose you, and appointed you, what for? 'That ye should go and bear fruit, and that your fruit should abide; that whatsoever ye ask of the Father in My name, He may give it you.'. . . I chose you in order to bear fruit, and in order that you may do so, I chose you to ask, and so to get into touch with God, that fruit may abound." (*The Gospel According to John,* p. 256)

Dr. Julius R. Mantey, the Greek grammarian and late professor in the Northern Baptist Theological Seminary, said on this verse: "The purpose of the Lord's choice was not for themselves alone; it was for others—*that ye should go and bear fruit.* This verse continues the imagery of the vine and the vintage. The purpose of discipleship and that of the grapevine are identical; both are to produce. Each is to reproduce his kind. This means that by 'bearing fruit' we help bring into being other disciples." (*The Evangelical Commentary,* "The Gospel of John," p. 304)

In the same commentary Dr. G. A. Turner observed, "They are chosen to serve. The choice is primarily here for service rather than for salvation. The initiative comes from the Lord. It is He who sends forth laborers into the vineyard, but His initiative is linked with human compliance with the command to pray." (*Ibid.*, p. 307)

Milligan and Moulton, in the *International Revision Commentary* are equally pronounced: "He had 'chosen' them—a choice having here nothing to do with eternal predestination, but only with choosing them out of the world after they were in it. He had 'appointed' them, and put them into the position which they were to occupy on their post of duty. . . . This can be nothing else but their going out into the world to take His place, to produce fruit to the glory of the Father, and to return with that fruit to their Father's house." ("John," pp. 327-328)

The Pulpit Commentary puts it this way: "I destined you to accomplish work dear to Me and essential to My kingdom. Christ has already told them . . . that 'severed' from Him they can 'do nothing.'. . . I appointed you as My apostles and representatives, to do work in My Name. . . . 'Fruit' would seem to be the abiding consequence of the 'greater works' which they would be called upon to do." (*The Pulpit Commentary*, "John," Vol. II, pp. 272-273)

Godet in his commentary on John believed this verse speaks of: "That work which constitutes the highest activity of which man can be judged worthy. By the term: *I have chosen you,* He alludes, as in 6:70 and 13:18, to the solemn act of their election to the apostleship. . . . The fruit designates here the communication to other men of the spiritual life which they themselves possess." (*John*, Vol. II, pp. 300-301)

It is no wonder, then, that Oliver B. Greene said: "John 15:16 was spoken to a group of men whom the Lord Jesus had chosen for a special ministry. God still chooses individuals to carry out a special ministry—but that has nothing to do with some being elected to be saved while others are not elected to be saved." (*Predestination*, p. 28)

Acts 2:23—"Him, being delivered by the determinate counsel and foreknowledge of God, ye have taken, and by wicked hands have crucified and slain."

Of course this verse is not speaking of men's relation to God nor an individual's salvation, but of God's fixed plan to provide the Redeemer for a lost world. Certainly, God had a plan, a sure plan, as prophesied. All fulfillment of prophecy rests on the same basis.

The statement means that God had decreed, determined beforehand, that His Son should be delivered (literally, given over) to the hands of men to do with as they would, which in their debased state would be to have Him destroyed (as they thought), but which God would turn, overrule, to the redemption of men.

We have heard it hastily concluded that the coupling of "determinate counsel *and* foreknowledge" shows that foreknowledge conveys the idea of purpose or determination. However, if that were the case, such joining of the terms would make the last word wholly unnecessary. Why should it be added if the thought were already expressed? That would be indiscriminate tautology; rather redundant for St. Peter to use under the circumstances of his address on this occasion.

In fact, the great Greek scholar, Dean Alford, commenting on this text (in words which we earlier quoted), said that these terms are *not* the same: "The counsel and foreknowledge of God are not to be joined . . . as if they were the agents—the connection in the original is that of accordance and appointment, not of agency. . . . The counsel and foreknowledge of God are not the same: the former designates His Eternal Plan, by which He has arranged all things (hence the determinate counsel)—the latter, the omniscience, by which every part of this plan is foreseen and unforgotten by Him." (*New Testament For English Readers,* Vol. I, Part II, p. 661)

Similarly, the European commentator, F. Godet, said: "In the passage Acts 2:23, foreknowledge is expressly distinguished from the fixed decree, and consequently can denote nothing but prescience; and as to 11:2: 'His people whom God foreknew,' the idea of knowledge is the leading one in the word foreknow." (*Commentary on the Romans,* Vol. II, pp. 108-109)

Notice, furthermore, that the last half of the verse shows the other side of the picture; it speaks of the corresponding part played by man. And it entirely holds up human responsibility. It is not lenient with those responsible for the death of Christ; it does not excuse them for their actions because they were playing a part in the great plan of God. Taken with other references to their deed (Acts 3:13-15; 5:30; 7:52c; 13:27-28; Luke 22:22) it shows that they were thoroughly culpable. As has sometimes been said, if they were acting only because God had pre-ordained that they should so act, they should not have been blamed; in fact, they should have been commended, they should have been rewarded for doing just what God willed. But such is not the tenor of the record.

Dr. C. Wordsworth said in his *Greek Testament with Notes*: "In order that they may not imagine that they have triumphed over God, and conquered Christ by the crucifixion, he says that it was done with the divine counsel. . . . But, in order that they may not therefore think themselves innocent, he adds, by wicked hands. Cp. 3:18; 4:28." ("Acts," p. 48)

Turning to the last reference cited by Dr. Wordsworth, we read his comment: "God decreed the salvation of the world by Christ, but He did not command or approve the means by which that consummation was brought about. . . . In all discussions on this and other similar texts we must not lose sight of certain great principles. 1. That God is the One Great First Cause. 2. That He wills that all should act according to the Law which He has given them. 3. That it is His will that man's will should be free." (*Ibid.*, p. 57)

Somewhat similarly, Dr. Harry Ironside said on this: "Notice how two things come together here that often trouble thinkers among men. First, God's predetermined purpose and wicked man's free will. God had predetermined that His blessed Son was to come into the world and give His life a ransom for sinners. . . . But God had not predetermined that men should curse Him, spit upon Him, and heap every kind of indignity upon Him. These things were of men's godlessness led on by Satan. Peter says, 'God sent Him; God knew all that would take place; but you are responsible for your sins in that you laid hold of Him and with your wicked hands crucified and slew Him.' " (*Lectures on Acts,* pp. 56-57)

Dr. R. E. Neighbour commented on this: "The fact that Jesus Christ was delivered by God and crucified according to the purpose of God, in no sense excused the villainy and sin of the men who were active in His crucifixion. Men took Him with wicked hands. God had purposed and promised that Christ should die the Just for the unjust; but the men who brought Him to Pilate and demanded His crucifixion were free moral agents. They acted on their own evil promptings. They were without excuse although they unwittingly provided themselves and all men with a possible Saviour. The blood of Christ was still upon their own hands." (*The Baptism of the Holy Ghost, or Before and After Pentecost.* An Exegesis of Acts 1 and 2. pp. 188-189)

Finally, Dr. G. Campbell Morgan elucidated this text: "It was murder; a vile murder; but it was more, infinitely more. It was something that took place 'by the determinate counsel and foreknowledge of God.' The Greek word translated 'determinate' here, is the word from which we derive our word 'horizon.' The phrase 'determinate counsel,' suggests the plan of God, that which was within the boundaries of His purpose.

The death of Jesus, said Peter in effect, was not an accident, not something brought about by men. It was the working out, in human history, and into visibility, of an eternal purpose and plan and power. But there was a human side to it, and Peter brought all the guilty face to face with the Cross." (*The Acts of the Apostles,* pp. 64-65)

Acts 13:48—"As many as were ordained to eternal life believed."

The word "ordained" here is not the usual term given that meaning. Dean Alford rendered it "as many as were disposed to eternal life," and then added: "The meaning of this word *disposed* must be determined by the context. The Jews had judged themselves unworthy of eternal life (verse 46); the Gentiles, as many as were disposed to eternal life, believed. By whom so disposed, is not here declared." Then after speaking of the initial part played by God, he said: "to find in this text pre-ordination to life asserted, is to force both the word and the context to a meaning which they do not contain." (*New Testament for English Readers,* Vol. I, Part II, p. 745)

J. R. Lumby in *The Cambridge Bible* said of this text: "In the controversies on predestination and election this sentence has constantly been brought forward. But it is manifestly unfair to take a sentence out of its context, and interpret it as if it stood alone. In verse 46 we are told that the Jews had judged themselves unworthy of eternal life, and all that is meant by the words in this verse is the opposite of that expression. The Jews were acting so as to proclaim themselves unworthy; the Gentiles were making manifest their desire to be deemed worthy." (*The Acts of The Apostles,* p. 168)

Similar to these are the comments by R. J. Knowling in

The Expositor's Greek Testament: "There is no countenance here for the *absolutum decretum* of the Calvinists, since verse 46 had already shown that the Jews had acted through their own choice. The words are really nothing more than a corollary of St. Paul's *anagkaion* ('necessary,' verse 46): the Jews as a nation had been ordained to eternal life—they had rejected this election—but those who believed amongst the Gentiles were equally ordained of God to eternal life, and it was according to His divine appointment that the apostles had turned to them." ("The Acts," p. 300)

More recently, the great Greek scholar Dr. A. T. Robertson said: "Why these Gentiles here ranged themselves on God's side as opposed to the Jews Luke does not tell us. This verse does not solve the vexed problem of divine sovereignty and human free agency. There is no evidence that Luke had in mind an *absolutum decretum* of personal salvation." (*Word Pictures in the New Testament,* The Acts, p. 200)

R. B. Rackham, in his commentary on Acts, which has gone through many editions, said: "Those who believed are described by St. Luke as those who *were ordained to eternal life.* These words have been wrested to teach the doctrine of predestination in a rigorous sense which they do not necessarily bear." Then, giving the terms a military sense which many relate to them, he paraphrased it, they "*had marshalled themselves* on the side of, or rather with a view to capture, eternal life." (*The Acts of the Apostles,* p. 221)

Alexander Maclaren in his *Expositions of Holy Scripture* said: "The din of many a theological battle has raged round these words, the writer of which would have probably needed a good deal of instruction before he could have been made to understand what the fight was about. . . . It would seem much more relevant and accordant with the context to understand the word rendered 'ordained' as meaning 'adapted' or 'fitted,' than to find in it a reference to divine foreordination. . . . The reference then would be to the 'frame of mind of the heathen, and not to the decrees of God.' " ("Acts," Vol. II, p. 48)

That great defender of the faith and champion of fundamentalism, the late Leander S. Keyser, said of this text: "We confess that, when we first read it, we could not help feeling that here, at last, was one passage that clearly teaches the divine election to be the cause and antecedent of faith. But it is never safe to jump to conclusions. So we determined to look up the Greek for the word 'ordained.' Not a little was our surprise. . . . Our classical dictionary (Liddell and Scott) does not give 'ordain' or 'foreordination' among them. . . . Let us give a literal translation of this part of the verse, putting the words in the precise order of the original: 'And they believed, as many as were arranged, settled, or made steady unto life eternal.' The meaning might easily be that God had made them steady unto eternal life through their faith. There may not be the least reference here to an eternal decree." (*Election and Conversion,* pp. 129-130)

As to Dr. Keyser's suggested order of the words in the verse (the "believed" coming first), we find it confirmed by W. E. Vine in his *Expository Dictionary of New Testament Words,* where he said under the term rendered "ordained," "It is said of those who, having believed the gospel, 'were ordained to eternal life,' Acts 13:48." (Vol. I, p. 68)

The afore quoted Dean Alford called attention to what "Dr. Wordsworth well observes" under this text: "It would be interesting to inquire, What influence these renderings in the *Vulgate Version* ('pre-ordained') had on the minds of some, like St. Augustine and his followers in the western church, in treating the great questions of free will, election, reprobation, and final perseverance? What also was the result of that influence on the minds of some writers of the Reformed Churches, who rejected the authority of Rome, which almost canonized that version; and yet in these two important texts (Acts 2:47; 13:48) were swayed away by it from the sense of the original? The tendency of the eastern fathers, who read the original Greek, was in a different direction from that of the western school; and Calvinism can receive no support from these two texts as they stand in the original words of inspiration, and as they were expounded by the primitive Church." (*The New Testament in the Original Greek, with Introduction and Notes,* by Chr. Wordsworth, "The Acts," p. 108)

Acts 16:14—"A certain woman named Lydia . . . whose heart the Lord opened, that she attended unto the things which were spoken of Paul."

These words, quite evidently are an *ex post facto* statement. Indeed, while we ourselves believe that we freely exercised faith in accepting the gospel, as we look back at it we would most gladly say that surely the Lord opened our heart to it. There admittedly is a divine and a human side. The verse before us presents the divine side. It does not deny the human side.

If anyone wants to be strict about what is in the verse, be it noted that *before* it is recorded that the Lord "opened her heart," it is said that she "heard us." Conceivably she could at once have refused to do just that, and that would have been the end of the matter for her.

Underscoring the two sides in this matter, the *Pulpit Commentary* points out, "It is well observed by Chrysostom, on the latter part of this verse, 'The opening of the heart was God's work, the attending was hers: so that it was both God's doing and man's.' " ("Acts of the Apostles," Vol. II, p. 29)

Many commentaries point out that Lydia was not a heathen, but a Jewish proselyte, one who "worshiped God" (recorded before the opening of the heart), and they then rest the case by comparing the expression here with the similar one in Luke 24:45 where two of the disciples, early believers, experienced the same thing.

Dr. J. M. Stifler commented on this incident as follows:

"Luke gives us a conception of the Christian which he had not presented before. From the beginning of the book there are three stages in this matter. At first we read, they who receive the Word, or, they believed. The next stage was, as many as were ordained to eternal life believed, or, God did visit the Gentiles to take out of them a people. Here it is, God opened the heart that Lydia might believe. There is no contradiction in the book on this point, but there is development. In noting the work of the risen Lord it was first observed that men believed. It was not long until it was seen that this belief was confined to certain individuals. And now it is learned that when those individuals believe, God's Spirit is acting upon their heart." (*An Introduction to the Book of Acts,* p. 154)

Romans 3:11—"There is none that seeketh after God."

This statement, it is assumed, shows that no man really ever exercises choice in the matter of coming to God or embracing His salvation.

This phrase is in a quotation from Psalm 14:2 and 53:2. It speaks of the fool and of those who have corrupted their way upon the earth. In Romans it is employed to give weight to the terrible indictment of man in his condition in sin.

Showing the use of the Old Testament verses quoted in this and the adjoining verses in Romans 3, Dr. Griffith Thomas said: "A reference to the contexts of these passages will show that the apostle does not mean to charge every individual Jew and Gentile with these sins. . . . The reference is of course to classes and tendencies of sin whether among Jews or Gentiles." (*Epistle to the Romans,* Vol. I, p. 126)

Since there are so many passages that speak of those who do seek God, and others that show that man should seek God, this statement obviously is to be understood as showing that there are none who seek God in the fullest sense or wholly as they should; in his corrupt human nature man has failed here as everywhere else.

A glance at a concordance will disclose the many who "sought" or were "seeking" the Lord, and in so doing were favorably spoken of. Furthermore, the divine injunctions to "seek" the Lord are clear. "Seek ye the Lord while He may be found, call ye upon Him while He is near" (Isaiah 55:6). "And ye shall seek Me, and find Me, when ye shall search for Me with all your heart" (Jeremiah 29:13). "That they should seek the Lord, if haply they might feel after Him, and find Him" (Acts 17:27). "He that cometh to God must believe that He is, and that He is a rewarder of them that diligently seek Him" (Hebrews 11:6). Surely the Lord does not tell man to do something which he is utterly incapable of doing.

Robert Haldane said on Romans: "During the whole course of our life God proposes Himself as the object that men are to seek (Isaiah 55:6), for the present is the time of His calling them, and if they do not find Him, it is owing to their perversity, which causes them to flee from Him, or to seek Him in a wrong way." (*Exposition of the Epistle to the Romans,* p. 118)

In his famous commentary on Romans, Martin Luther said on this verse: "They do not seek after God as He desires to be sought and found, namely, not by human wisdom and searching, but by faith and in humility. . . . We must continuously seek after Him; indeed, we must seek Him evermore, as the Psalmist says in Psalm 105:4: 'Seek the Lord . . . seek His face evermore.' " (*Commentary on the Epistle to the Romans,* translated by J. T. Mueller, pp. 54-55)

Dr. Frederic W. Farr, previously cited, said: "Ezekiel 18:31-32, etc. Sinners are commanded to make themselves a new heart. This is their perpetual duty. Therefore, it must be in the power of the will, since ability is the measurement of obligation." (*A Manual of Christian Doctrine,* p. 76)

B. H. Carroll said: "The true penitent is a seeker and a

striver after eternal life. He is no inert mass, but a vitalized, energized, active intelligence. The Bible does not describe him as a dumb, uninterested, stupid man, waiting for irresistible force to drag him into Heaven by the hair of the head. It represents him rather as 'fleeing from the wrath to come,' and 'laying hold of the hope set before him.' " (*Sermons,* p. 204)

See also C. H. Spurgeon's sermon on 1 Chronicles 28:9: "If thou seek Him, He will be found of thee," in the first sentence of which he says his text may be "addressed to every unconverted person here present, for there are a great many texts of Scripture of a similar import which apply to all ungodly ones."

Or read D. L. Moody's sermon, "Sinners Seeking Christ" (*Select Sermons,* pp. 75-85) or George W. Truett's sermon, "Seeking and Finding." (*The Prophet's Mantle,* pp. 183-194)

Romans 8:29-30—"For whom He did foreknow, He also did predestinate . . . whom He did predestinate, them He also called."

This is one of only two chapters in the New Testament where the word predestinate is found. This text has been largely dealt with under the previous section, "That To Which Predestination and Election Refer," quoting H. A. Ironside, A. T. Robertson, I. M. Haldeman, W. L. Pettingill, M. G. Cambron, C. H. Spurgeon, etc.

By way of supplementing what has earlier been said, the following may also aid in understanding this passage.

H. A. Ironside pointed out: "God by His foreknowledge has predestinated all who believe in the Lord Jesus Christ 'to be conformed to the image of His Son' (Romans 8:29). Predestination is never to Heaven, nor yet to hell; but always to special privilege in and with Christ. . . . The gospel preacher can declare without any kind of mental reservation the blessed fact that whosoever will, may take the water of life freely (Revelation 22:17). This is not at all a question of being allowed to take Christ as Saviour. It is an earnest entreaty to do so." (*What's The Answer?*, pp. 43-44)

The same writer said in his *Lectures on Romans:* "We have been predestinated to become fully like our blessed Lord—'conformed to the image of God's Son,' that He, who was from all eternity the 'only Begotten,' might be 'the Firstborn among many brethren.' " (p. 106)

Dr. Robert C. McQuilkin, late president of Columbia Bible College, who taught Romans for over twenty years, pointed out: "There follows a summing up of God's eternal purpose for everyone who is saved. . . . Each one of these has been foreordained or predetermined by God's plan for each one. . . . When we have a body like Christ, then is our redemption complete. We are glorified. Since no one is yet glorified, we can see clearly that these words are not speaking of something that has been done, but describing what is God's plan and what is the process for every saved man." (*The Message of Romans, An Exposition,* pp. 105-106)

Dr. H. E. Jacobs who wrote the popular Lutheran Commentary on Romans, summarized what is there brought out on this passage, in his book on theology: "Does not Romans 8:30, 'Whom He predestinated, them He also called,' restrict the call to a class, viz., to those predestinated from all eternity, and ultimately 'glorified'? No. Paul does not say that none were called except the predestinated, or none were called except the justified; but he exhibits the succession of acts through which those at last glorified are brought to salvation." (*A Summary of The Christian Faith,* p. 217)

Bishop Wordsworth has extensive comments on these verses, on which he said, in part: "The apostle's purpose here is to teach the Jews that they may not presume upon being God's people, on the ground of His *foreknowledge,* unless they obey His *call* to them in Christ; and that all are God's people who imitate the *faith* of Abraham, and accept the gospel of Christ. . . . It must be borne in mind that Holy Scripture, in order to produce more assurance in us, often describes things as *done* which God desires *should be done*. . . . God is not willing that any should perish (2 Peter 3:9), but will have all men to be saved (1 Timothy 2:4). He shut up all under sin in order that He might have mercy upon all (Romans 11:32). . . . He gave Himself a ransom for all men (1 Timothy 2:6). He died for all (2 Corinthians 5:14-15). . . . The grace of God that bringeth salvation hath appeared to all men (Titus 2:11). . . . In order also to guard against any narrow interpretations of this particular passage, St. Paul expressly declares here that God spared not His own Son, but gave Him up to death for us all (verse 32). . . . It would have been no encouragement to them to tell them that God had only called an unknown few among them. It would be inconsistent with, and in contradiction to the whole scope of the apostle in this Epistle, to suppose that God limits His offers to a few. The main drift of St. Paul in the present Epistle, is to eradicate such a notion from the mind of the Jews, who imagined that God's favors were confined to themselves; and to show the universality of God's love in Christ." (*Greek Testament, With Notes,* "Romans," p. 242)

We might appropriately quote Dr. Griffith Thomas, who said in his *Epistle to the Romans:* "The fact that they love God (verse 28) implies and presupposes His dealings with them in several definite stages or links in the chain of His relationship, all of which will be realized in due time. They were foreknown. . . . He foreordained them to be conformed to the image of His Son. . . . They were glorified. Thus the work was completed and crowned and salvation fully realized. . . . No vicissitudes can possibly rob believers of their eternal glory. Of course we must not forget that in other passages the human side and the various human conditions of this complete work are equally clearly brought to our notice." (Vol. II, pp. 95-97)

We have already quoted Pastor Edward Drew on the first

part of these verses where he shows the goal of predestination. He wrote, on the final part of these verses: "Now for some unknown reason we put all of this in the past, and we take a verse like this and say that only those whom the Lord called could come to Him. He called everyone. This word 'called' in the 30th verse is a form of the word used only eleven times in the New Testament, and in no place is it necessary to put it in the past. It is a word that can be translated 'called out.' After the Lord saved you He called you out, because you are distinctly His. The Lord's people are called-out ones. . . . Let me say that if you will take the eleven places in the New Testament where this word is used in this form, and translate it 'called out,' you will get the true sense." (*Studies in the Book of Romans,* Sermon on Romans 8:29-32, March 1, 1942)

Romans 9–11.

These chapters have been quite perplexing to many. In them there seems to be set forth a system of rigid predetermination, and more, the justice and fairness of God in dealing with human beings appears to be left in question. To some, these chapters have been assumed to settle the matter of every man being placed wholly within a strict pattern worked out in the long distant past. But more may have been read into them than is rightly seen to be there. Well-known students of the Word have fully analyzed these passages in harmony with their main theme and called attention to their real significance. Some citations may prove helpful.

Because of the extended portion of Scripture dealt with here, and because of its crucial nature, we give more space to this than we have to other texts. First, we aim to take up the general nature of these chapters, and then come back to deal with special points, such as that of Jacob and Esau, Pharaoh, the potter and the clay, or vessels of wrath, etc.

As to the central point of these chapters, H. H. Halley in his well-known *Bible Handbook* pointed out: "While considerable numbers of Jews had become Christians, yet the nation as a whole was not only unbelieving but bitterly antagonistic. . . . It was Jewish unbelievers that made trouble for Paul in almost every place he went. If Jesus was really the Messiah of their own Scripture prophecy, how does it happen that God's own nation has thus rejected Him? In these three chapters is Paul's answer. . . . Paul is not discussing the predestination of individuals to salvation or condemnation, but is asserting God's absolute sovereignty in the choice and management of nations for world functions." (Seventeenth edition, p. 527)

In his *Lectures on Romans* H. A. Ironside said: "Many godly Jews . . . were passing through a time of great perplexity and bewilderment as they saw their own nation apparently hardened into opposition against the gospel, and sinners of the Gentiles turning to the Lord. . . . In the three chapters that are now to occupy us, the apostle meets this question, and that in a masterly way, showing how the righteousness of God is harmonized with His dispensational ways. . . . There is no question here of predestination to Heaven or reprobation to hell; in fact, eternal issues do not really come in throughout this chapter. . . . We are not told here, nor anywhere else, that before children are born it is God's purpose to send one to Heaven and another to hell. . . . The passage has to do entirely with privilege here on earth." (pp. 109-110,116)

On this J. Sidlow Baxter said: "As to the scope of the passage, it will become obvious that it is all about God's dealings with men and nations historically and dispensationally, and is *not* about individual salvation and destiny beyond the grave. Now that is the absolutely vital fact to remember in reading the problem verses of these chapters. John Calvin is wrong when he reads into these verses election either to salvation or to damnation in the eternal sense. That is not their scope. They belong only to a divine economy of history. . . . Let us further say that God could never create any man either to be wicked or to be eternally damned. 'Is there unrighteousness with God? God forbid!' In Romans 9 we simply must not read an after-death significance into what is solely historical." (*Explore the Book,* Vol. VI, pp. 88-89)

Similarly, of this section of Romans, Sanday and Headlam said: "We must not read into it more than it contains: as, for example, Calvin does. He imports various extraneous ideas. . . . The apostle says nothing about eternal life or death." (*International Critical Commentary,* "Romans," p. 258)

On these chapters M. R. Vincent said: "These chapters, as they are the most difficult of Paul's writings, have been most misunderstood and misapplied. Their most dangerous perversion is that which draws from them the doctrine of God's arbitrary predestination of individuals to eternal life or eternal perdition. It can be shown that such is not the intent of these chapters. They do not discuss the doctrine of individual election and reprobation with reference to eternal destiny. . . . The discussion in these three chapters . . . is aimed at the Jews' national and religious conceit. It is designed to show them that, notwithstanding their claim to be God's elect people, the great mass of their nation has been justly rejected by God; and further that God's elective purpose includes the Gentiles. Hence, while maintaining the truth of divine sovereignty in the strongest and most positive manner, it treats it on a grander scale, and brings it to bear against the very elect themselves. . . . The truths of divine sovereignty and elective freedom require to be presented in their most absolute aspect as against man's right to dictate to God. The parallel facts of man's free agency and consequent responsibility, which are equally patent in these chapters, are, at certain points, thrown into the shade; so that, if the attention is fastened upon particular passages or groups of passages, the result will be a one-sided and untruthful conception of the divine economy, which may easily run into a challenge of God's justice and benevolence." (*Word Studies in the New Testament,* Vol. III, pp. 133-135)

In his rich and rather full commentary on Romans, Dr. Griffith Thomas pointed up the import of this portion: "Here he (the Jew) is considered nationally, and in relation to the whole world. . . . The one problem all through is how God can reject those whom He has elected [!!], and this question is met." (Exclamation ours.) Then he continued: "The failure of Israel was due, not to any compulsion on the part of God, but to their own attitude of willful disobedience to God and His gospel. . . . The main line of thought is national rather than individual. . . . He (the apostle) shows that rejection of the Jews is due to their rejection of the gospel, for if God had been arbitrary He would have been unjust, and yet He is not unjust. . . . The primary thought of the apostle in these chapters is not individual salvation, but the philosophy of history. . . . Israel's election had for its object the service of his fellow men. St. Paul is concerned not so much with individuals, as with nations and masses of people. He speaks of God's choice of Israel, not to eternal life as such, but to privileges and duty. . . . God's chosen men are His 'choice' men. . . ." (*Romans, A Devotional Commentary,* Vol. II, pp. 115-116,156-157,222,228-229)

One more citation comes from a scholarly source. Bishop Wordsworth stated: "When these chapters are considered in their natural relation to the apostle's design in this Epistle, it will be seen that it was no part of his purpose to discuss here the question of the particular predestination of *individuals.* . . . The Calvinistic interpretations of this chapter fail altogether of supplying any answer to the objections of the Jew, or of ministering any comfort to him in his dejection; from which he can only be raised by the blessed assurance with which St. Paul concludes this chapter, that 'he that believeth in Christ shall not be put to shame.' Consequently we find that the great body of ancient expositors, in commenting on this portion of St. Paul's Epistle, never assigned to it such a meaning as has been imputed to it by some in more recent times. Indeed, the ancient expositors regarded this Epistle generally, and this portion of it particularly, as a storehouse of divine teaching on the great doctrine of *universal redemption,* and of *free grace* offered to *all* in Christ." (Emphasis his. *Greek Testament With Notes,* "Romans," p. 246)

Romans 9:10-13—"For the children being not yet born . . . it is written, Jacob have I loved, but Esau have I hated."

These phrases are often taken in a fragmented manner. Consider them in the light of the context and in the light of God's entire revelation.

Dr. Griffith Thomas pointed out: "It should be carefully noted that St. Paul is referring to the seed of Abraham typically and spiritually (cf. Galatians 4:29). . . . The reference is, of course, to Jacob and Esau in their national capacity, and not to any 'hate' of Esau while yet unborn. . . . It is therefore no question of personal salvation by absolute decree." (*Romans,* Vol. II, p. 133-134)

Following on, Dr. Ironside declared: "Be it observed that it was not before the children were born, neither had done any good or evil, that God said, 'Jacob have I loved, but Esau have I hated.' These words are quoted from the very last book of the Old Testament. We find them in Malachi. . . . Dispensationally, Jacob was loved, Esau hated. There is no reference to the individual as such. 'God so loved the world,' and therefore every child of Jacob or Esau may be saved who will." (*Lectures on Romans,* p. 117-118)

The noted writer, Dr. L. S. Keyser, said on these verses: "Paul teaches that not all the seed of Abraham was elected to be the bearers of God's saving plan. . . . Does this prove that

God unconditionally elected Jacob unto salvation and passed Esau by? Not at all. . . . These two men were treated as the representatives of their respective posterities. . . . With reference to God's loving Jacob and hating Esau, we will defer to Dr. Jacobs (Lutheran Commentary, *in loco,* p. 190): 'The word hatred here does not mean to dislike or abhor. It simply expresses the preference shown to one who is loved when his claims or interests come in conflict with the other. . . . "When a Hebrew compares a less with a greater love, he is wont to call the former hatred." (Tholuck).' " (*Election and Conversion,* pp. 119-120)

Similarly, Dr. H. C. Thiessen said: "The choice of Jacob rather than Esau was at most a choice to outward and national privilege; it was not a choice to salvation directly. No doubt God, in foreseeing that Jacob and his descendents would much more fully than Esau and his descendents choose the things of spiritual value, chose Jacob for the covenant relationship which he and his descendents later came to enjoy. . . . A descendent of Esau could, no doubt, be saved as readily as a descendent of Jacob." (*Lectures in Systematic Theology,* pp. 348-349)

It is no wonder, then, that Pastor Edward Drew said: "Here and anywhere else that you have predestination and election, it is not to salvation. Nowhere does the Bible say that God has chosen this one to be saved and that one to be lost. This is not salvation. This is service. Let me show you that. Romans 9:12—*The elder shall serve the younger.* That is not salvation. . . . God didn't do *that* before they were born. That is a quotation from Malachi, and Malachi is the last book of the Old Testament, written a thousand years after these two men lived. God did not say before they were born that He loved one and hated the other; but when one went against God, having the birthright and blessing, and holding them so loosely that he lost them and didn't want what God had to give him, then he incurred the hatred of God. Jacob, to whom belonged nothing, wanted everything God had to give." (*Studies in the Book of Romans,* Sermon, Sunday, March 22, 1942)

Romans 9:16—"So then it is not of him that willeth, nor of him that runneth, but of God that sheweth mercy."

This text appears to state conclusively that the human element plays no part in man's relation to God. The will here seems to be entirely set aside.

But it is necessary to note carefully that to which reference is being made. To what does the third word, "it," refer? Not to man's salvation or his approach to God. The exegetes point out that the "it" refers to God's showing mercy. The subject is in the previous verse where it points to God saying, "I will have mercy on whom I will have mercy." And the last phrase of this verse says, "but of God that sheweth mercy." So it is the extending of divine mercy that is not "of him that willeth." Certainly, mercy toward a fallen race is of God, not man, and none of us deserves it. As pointed out earlier, we recognize that God takes the initiative in the redemption of the race; without His first manifesting His mercy and grace toward lost sinners, there would be no salvation at all. This is also true of our service. We are utterly unworthy of His high calling, but in mercy He condescends to use us. At this we will never cease to marvel.

Some strongly Calvinistic commentators seem to infer the subject to be participation in God's mercy, but there appears to be no particular warrant for this any more than the other way, that of the extension of God's mercy to mankind. Indeed, for the latter there is scriptural ground, and right in the context where, in carrying out the theme of this section, we read in chapter 11:32, "God hath concluded them all in unbelief, that He might have mercy upon all."

Dr. Griffith Thomas pointed to God's mercy as the subject and its extension to the Gentiles in comparison with its previous relation to Israel as the theme of this section: "God's mercy (verse 16) is not merely a response to human resolve ('him that willeth'), or to human effort ('him that runneth'). His own divine will is the one and only source of His mercy. All men are sinners, and as God pardoned Israel when they were rebels, why may He not pardon the Gentiles also?" (Parenthesis his. *Epistle to the Romans,* Vol. II, p. 140)

J. M. Stifler on Romans, said: "God's mercy is not the response to human desire nor to human effort. It is not of him that 'willeth' or wishes it, as Moses did, and not of him who 'runneth' in the path of right. Willing and running may indicate the possession of grace, but they are not the originating cause. They may be the channel, but they are not the fountain." (p. 172)

H. A. Ironside commented on this text: "He is not setting aside the will of man; he is not declaring that no responsibility to run in the way of righteousness rests upon man; but he *is* declaring that, apart from the sovereign mercy of God, no man would ever will to be saved or run in the way of His commandments." (*Lectures on Romans,* p. 120)

Bishop Moule in the *Cambridge Bible for Schools* said: "Not that human willing and running are illusions; but they are not the *cause* of the mercy. They follow it; they may even be the channel of its present action; but they are not the cause." (*Epistle to the Romans,* p. 170)

On this Dr. L. S. Keyser said: "As we have shown all along–God is the enabling source of all good, of the willing and the running. But remember He will not do our willing and running for us, after He has conferred the ability upon us through His mercy and grace." (*Election and Conversion,* p. 121)

Romans 9:17-18—"Pharaoh . . . and whom He will He hardeneth."

One prominent writer, a Baptist, said, "To my own mind, Romans 9:18 has been the most disturbing verse in the Bible. It easily seems to suggest that what we call the sovereignty of God is an unspeakably awful divine despotism." But an answer may readily be found, and that writer is one of those we quote below.

On these verses Dr. J. Sidlow Baxter said: "The awesome words to Pharaoh can be faced in their full force—'Even for this same purpose have I raised thee up, that I might show My power in thee, and that My name might be declared throughout all the earth.' The words 'raised thee up' do not mean that God had raised him up from *birth* for this purpose: they refer to his elevation to the highest throne on earth. Nay, as they occur in Exodus 9:16, they scarce mean even *that,* but only that God had kept Pharaoh from dying in the preceding plague, so as to be made the more fully an object lesson to all men. Moreover, when Paul (still alluding to Pharaoh) says, 'And whom He will, He hardeneth' (verse 18), we need not try to soften the word. God did not override Pharaoh's own will. The hardening was a reciprocal process. Eighteen times we are told that Pharaoh's heart was 'hardened' in refusal. In about half of these the hardening is attributed to Pharaoh himself; in the others to God. But the whole contest between God and Pharaoh must be interpreted by what God said to Moses before ever the contest started: 'The king of Egypt *will not*' (Exodus 3:19). The will was already set. The heart was already hard. The hardening process developed inasmuch as the plagues forced Pharaoh to an issue which crystallized his sin. . . . Pharaoh's *eternal* destiny is not the thing in question." (Emphasis his. *Explore the Book,* Vol. VI, pp. 88-89)

On these same verses, Pastor Edward Drew said: "That is God's purpose in the nations. God didn't say to Moses, 'I have chosen Pharaoh, and I am going to send him to hell.' He didn't say that. The Scripture says that God hardened Pharaoh's heart, but God didn't harden Pharaoh's heart until Moses went to him and said, 'God says, "Let My people go,"' and Pharaoh said, 'Who is God that I should obey Him?' Then began the process of hardening his heart. . . . God let Pharaoh work out His purposes, and Israel was delivered. The purposes of God are never hindered." (*Studies in the Book of Romans,* as noted.)

In his commentary, Dr. Griffith Thomas said: "This would be an argument exactly suited to the Jewish objector. God was only acting upon the same principle as He acted upon in regard to Pharaoh when He hardened unbelieving Israel. But although the apostle's words are adequate to meet the purely Jewish objection, the problem is acute for us today who read this reference to Pharaoh. It does not mean that Pharaoh was hardened for the mere sake of hardening, for we are told ten times in Exodus of Pharaoh hardening himself. He is used here as an illustration of divine power as manifested and revealed in the outcome of the monarch's self-will and hardening of his own heart. 'I raised thee up,' does not mean that he was created for the purpose of being hardened, but as Denney renders it, 'Brought thee on the stage of history.' It simply states that God brought about everything that belonged to Pharaoh's history, even though Pharoah himself was perfectly free in his action. . . . Pharaoh's heart was hardened by means of divine displays of power that were fitted and intended to have a precisely opposite effect. . . . We know from the history that it was Pharaoh's disobedience alone that led to his being hardened. Neither Pharaoh nor anyone else is ever created in order to be hardened." (*Epistle to the Romans,* Vol. II, pp. 141-143)

Showing the nature of the case here, M. R. Vincent said: "Persistent disobedience and resistance, working their natural result of inflated pride and presumptuous foolhardiness, wrought out a condition of heart which invited and insured judgment. . . . The operation of these forces did not exclude moral agency or moral freedom. No irresistible constraint compelled Pharaoh to yield to this pressure toward evil. His power of choice was recognized, assumed, and appealed to. . . . God's dealing with Pharaoh was marked by forbearance, opportunities for repentance, instruction, and chastisement." (*Word Studies in the New Testament,* Vol. III, pp. 141-143)

In his Spurgeon's College lectures, H. H. Rowley said: "These passages would seem to suggest that Pharaoh's refusal to let the Israelites go was something for which not he but God was responsible, and he was but executing the will of God in all that he did. Such a view on the face of it would make nonsense of the whole story. . . . That Pharaoh is not thought of as a mere puppet is made quite clear by the passages which state that Pharaoh hardened his own heart. His act was none the less his own because God could use it. . . . Pharaoh served the purpose of God, and for the iniquity of his harshness, which aroused God's pity, he bears the full responsibility and cannot escape condemnation." (*The Biblical Doctrine of Election,* pp. 132-133)

Romans 9:19-23—"Hath not the potter power over the clay . . . vessels of wrath fitted to destruction."

Dr. Griffith Thomas said on these verses: "This illustration, together with the word 'formed' rather than 'created' in verse 20, deserves attention, as showing the apostle is not referring to original creation, but to spiritual destination. God is regarded as taking men as He finds them, just as the potter does not create the clay but uses it. . . . The 'vessels of wrath' are described generally as 'fitted to destruction,' that is, fitted by themselves, through their own sin. Men fit themselves for hell, but it is God that fits them for Heaven.

. . . The figure of the potter and the clay must not be overpressed, since man has a will which the clay has not. The figure does not cover the entire relationship of God to man. . . . Paul is treating of God's right to harden an already unbelieving and disobedient people." (*Epistle to the Romans,* Vol. II, pp. 147-148,153-154)

Confirming Dr. Thomas's setting forth "fitted themselves," we find W. E. Vine in his *Expository Dictionary of New Testament Words* saying of "destruction": "metaphorically of men persistent in evil (Romans 9:22), where 'fitted' is in the middle voice, indicating that the vessels of wrath fitted themselves for destruction." (Vol. I, pp. 303-304)

Dr. Ironside commented on these verses: "Beginning with verse 19, the apostle undertakes to meet the objection of the fatalist, the man who says, 'Well, granting all you've been saying, then God's decrees are irresistible. . . . What ground can there be for judgment of a creature who can never will, nor run, but as God Himself directs? To resist His will is impossible. Where, then, does moral responsibility come in?' Such objections to the doctrine of divine sovereignty have been raised from the earliest days. But inasmuch as we have already seen that the apostle simply has in view privilege here on earth, those objections fall to the ground. The privileged Jew may fail utterly to appreciate the blessings lavished upon him, and so come under divine condemnation; while the ignorant barbarian may, nevertheless, have an exercised conscience that will lead him into the presence of God. . . . If God, the great Former of all, willing to manifest both His anger and His power, endures, with much long-suffering, vessels that call down His indignation because, having a will, which the work of the potter has not, they deliberately fit themselves for destruction, shall anyone find fault?" (*Lectures on Romans,* pp. 122-123)

B. H. Carroll, a Baptist of the South, even more strikingly said: "High above human thought, beyond the scope of human sight, of the human mind, the Omnipotence and

Omniscience is ruling, and His rule is supreme, and yet nobody is taken by the hair and dragged into hell, and nobody is taken by the hair and dragged into Heaven. Let us explain and give the application of the vessels of wrath and mercy. . . . Those that were vessels of wrath, those who voluntarily stand against God, God patiently endured a long time, and His forbearance signified that He was giving them opportunity for repentance. . . . If He had selected the Jewish nation, every one of them to be saved in Heaven, and rejected every other nation, then the objection would have been sustained, but it had a different purpose. The election of the Jewish nation looked to the salvation of the Jews and Gentiles that received the message of God." (*An Interpretation of the English Bible,* Vol. XIV, Galatians, Romans, etc., pp. 181-182)

Dr. H. H. Rowley commented on the potter and the clay: "It may be replied that there are passages in the Bible which suggest that God is arbitrary. There are, for instance, those passages which speak of Him under the metaphor of a potter, making now a vessel of honor, and now a vessel of dishonor, of the same lump of clay, or refashioning the clay at will. . . . But is the potter arbitrary in his work? Neither Jeremiah nor Paul had in mind an aimless dilettante, working in a casual and haphazard way, turning out vessels according to the chance whim of the moment. . . . When God destroys, He destroys because His purpose is not realized, and men are not serviceable to Him, and not because He created in order to destroy. . . . The notion of election to Heaven or hell men have introduced into the question. The vessel of dishonor is thought of as a child of hell. But this is really irrelevant to the meaning of either prophet or apostle. To suppose that a crazy potter, who made vessels with no other thought than that he would afterwards knock them to pieces, is the type and figure of God, is supremely dishonoring to God. The vessel of dishonor which the potter makes is still something that he wants, and that has a definite use. . . . The instruments of wrath . . . were what the New Testament calls 'vessels of dishonor,' serving God indeed, but with no exalted service. They were not puppets in His hand, compelled to do His will without moral responsibility for their deed, but chosen because He saw that the very iniquity of their heart would lead them to the course that He could use." (*The Biblical Doctrine of Election,* pp. 40-41,128)

M. R. Vincent says on this subject: "Man, on God's own showing, is not a lump of senseless clay. He is a sentient, reasoning being, endowed by God with the power of self-determination. God Himself cannot and does not treat him as a lump of clay; and to assert such a relation between God and man made in God's image, is to assert what is contrary to common sense and to God's own declarations and assumptions in Scripture. . . . By Old Testament passages the idea of God dealing with men as lifeless clay, shaping them to eternal life or death according to His arbitrary will, is contradicted. The illustration points away from God's causing unbelief, to God's bearing with man's voluntary and persistent disobedience, and to His making of him the best that can be made consistently with divine justice and holiness. So far from accentuating rigid narrowness of purpose, arbitrary and inexorable destination of individuals to honor or dishonor, the illustration opens a vast range and free play of divine purpose to turn evil to good. . . . God does not make men in order to destroy them. God ordains no man to eternal death. . . . The fact that men do become vessels unto dishonor, merely proves the power which God has lodged in the human will of modifying, and in a sense defeating, His sovereign purpose of love. He 'will have all men to be saved and come to a knowledge of truth'; yet Christ comes to His own, and His own receive Him not, and He weeps as He exclaims, 'Ye will not come unto Me, that ye might have life.'. . . Are you disposed to construe the words 'whom He will He hardeneth' into an assertion of the arbitrary, relentless, and unjust severity of God? '. . . endured. . .' Did not this endurance imply opportunity to repent, and assume that destruction was not God's arbitrary choice, but theirs?" (*Word Studies in the New Testament*, Vol. III, pp. 144,147-148)

Romans 9–11. Later portions and summary.

What has been presented from these chapters is perhaps enough to show how these problem passages may be understood. We cannot do better than to conclude in the words of others.

Dr. L. S. Keyser said: "We have dealt with the difficult passages in these chapters; and yet we wonder whether it was necessary to expend so much labor on them, when Paul himself afterward makes everything plain (9:30-32): 'What shall we say then?' Note his own answer: 'That the Gentiles who followed not after righteousness, attained to the righteousness, even the righteousness which is *of faith*; but Israel . . . sought it not *by faith* . . . he that *believeth* on Him shall not be put to shame.' There it all is, just as clear as crystal—just why God elects some and does not elect others. If we walk in this rich garden of truth in the light of justifying faith, which God has revealed to us in His Word, we shall not walk in darkness. . . . If it were necessary, we should take pleasure in going through chapters ten and eleven, to show how Paul again and again maintains that Israel was rejected for a time on account of their lack of faith, while many of the Gentiles were grafted in because they did not depend on their good works, but solely on faith; but we simply invite the reader to examine these luminous passages for himself." (Emphasis his. *Election and Conversion*, pp. 124-125)

On these chapters in Romans, H. H. Rowley commented: "With the thought of the limitation of the election of Israel to but a part of the Israel according to the flesh, he [Paul] combined the thought of the extension of that election beyond the bounds of the nation to those amongst the Gentiles who should come to share the faith and the task of Israel. . . . In the same Epistle [Romans] he speaks of some of the branches of the tree of Israel having been broken off through unbelief, and Gentiles being grafted in to take their place. It is of the grace and goodness of God that they are grafted in, and it can only be as they respond to that grace by faith that they can remain in the tree. . . . Paul warned the Romans not to glory over the branches which had been plucked from the tree of election, but to realize that if God had not spared those branches, neither would He spare the newly grafted ones, if they ceased to manifest true faithfulness unto Him. And loyalty to God always involves the discharge of the task which is the corollary of election." (*The Biblical Doctrine of Election,* pp. 144-145,166)

Again on these chapters Bishop Wordsworth put down: "St. Paul has shown that Christ had died *for all* (8:32); and that *all* who accept by faith the terms of salvation offered them in Christ, are the elect people of God; and that *all* the faithful had been foreknown by Him in Christ (8:29-32), and that He, on His part, gives them freely justification and salvation in Him." (*Greek Testament, with Notes,* p. 246)

In the introduction to this Epistle, Wordsworth said, God "gives grace in order to quicken our *will.* And He gives us reason, conscience, and Scripture, to guide it. It is also God's will that all they who freely accept the terms of salvation which are *freely* made by Him, should be saved; but that they who abuse their free will and reject what He offers, and what He desires them to accept, shall fail of salvation and incur punishment and perdition. . . . We must not fall into the Arminian error, which represents man's goodness, foreseen by God, as the ground of God's predestination of the godly. . . . Man's faith in God is indeed a *condition* of that predestination, but God's love to man in Christ is its cause. . . . If the Calvinistic interpretation of these chapters is applied to the solution of the questions, by which the Jews, with whom the apostle is arguing, pressed St. Paul, it will be found to be wholly inadequate to the purpose. Of little avail would it have been for him to assure the Jews (who supposed themselves to be God's elect), that some few, unknown persons, had been predestinated by God to salvation, under the gospel, and that all the rest of mankind had been eternally condemned as reprobates, and were doomed by an irresistible decree to eternal perdition. Yet this is the assertion which the Calvinistic interpretation imputes to St. Paul!" (*Ibid.*, pp. 197-198,199-200)

Ephesians 1:4-5,11—"Chosen us in Him before the foundation of the world . . . having predestinated us unto the adoption of children. . . ."

As many have pointed out, observe, first, the subjects of the choice, "us," believers, not the people of the world (the apostle includes himself); and secondly, the object or goal of predestination, "unto the adoption of children."

W. B. Riley said on this passage: "The term 'predestination' which has alarmed many, is only another expression of the eternal compassion, the eternal plan, the eternal purpose, the eternal project—redemption! The believer's position, however, is by the exercise of man's will. He has 'predestinated us unto the adoption of children. . .' but He will never foreclose on that which He has purchased without our personal consent. The day one is willing to be adopted, that day he becomes God's child. . . . Our adoption is done the moment we consent to it; but the joy of it all, to the praise and glory of His grace—comes to us in ever-increasing measure." (*The Bible of the Expositor and the Evangelist,* "New Testament," Vol. XII, pp. 13-15)

Another Baptist pastor and teacher, Dr. A. J. Wall, said on this: "One must first conclude that he is talking about saved persons and not the means of their salvation. Then in verses four and five as he talks about choosing and predestinating, he is talking about saved people, for Paul includes himself by saying 'us.'. . . It did not say 'according as He has chosen some to be saved before the foundation of the world,' but 'according as He hath chosen *us*' (we who are believers) . . . 'that we should be holy and without blame before Him in love.' Not that some should be saved or that some shall be lost, for the subject of the salvation of the soul is not mentioned. Before the foundation of the world God chose that the believers in Christ should be, or stand, before Christ in love, holy and without blame. It must be some future time when the believer will be conformed to the image of His Son. . . . Ephesians 1:11, the believer is predestinated to receive an inheritance that has already been purchased, obtained, or paid for." (*The Truth About Election*, pp. 12-14)

Dr. G. Campbell Morgan commented on these verses: "May God deliver us from taking so great, so stupendous and sublime and far-reaching a vision of the wisdom which transcends our finite theory, in order to formulate a doctrine that God has chosen a few people to be saved and left the rest to be damned. That is an unwarranted deduction.

"The plan of the Church existed in the mind of God from eternity. He predestined the Church," and note that it was the Church and not people of the world, "that it should be conformed to the image of His Son." (*Living Messages of the Books of The Bible,* "Matthew To Colossians," p. 172)

In *The Expositor's Bible,* G. G. Findlay brought out: "The divine prescience . . . as well as His absolute righteousness, forbids the treasonable thought of anything arbitrary or unfair cleaving to this predetermination–anything that should override our free will and make our responsibility an illusion. . . . He foresees everything and allows for everything. The consistence of foreknowledge with free will is an enigma which the apostle did not attempt to solve. . . . They are men devoted to God by their own choice and will, meeting God's choice and will for them. . . . Four times, in these three verses, with exulting emphasis, the apostle claims this distinction for 'us.' *Who*, then, are the objects of the primordial election of grace? Does St. Paul use the pronoun distributively, thinking of individuals . . . or does he mean the Church, as that is collectively the family of God and the object of His loving ordination? In this Epistle, the latter is surely the thought."

This same scholar renders the eleventh verse, "In whom also—i.e., Christ—we received our heritage, predestinated [to it], according to His purpose." (Brackets his. "Epistle to the Ephesians," pp. 28-33,42)

C. Wordsworth, in his *New Testament in the Original Greek, With Notes and Introductions,* wrote similarly: "Ignatius applies the words *election* and *predestination*—and he supposed St. Paul to apply them—to the whole visible Church of God at Ephesus; to all those who were joined together in the body of Christ. . . . St. Peter also (1 Peter 1:1-2) applies the words 'Elect according to the foreknowledge of God,' to the whole societies of Christians; and he applies the word 'co-elect' to a church (1 Peter 5:13). This observation might have preserved this text from becoming a subject of contentious controversy concerning the election and final reprobation of *individuals*. . . . Many times there is no reason known to us of God's acting; but, that there is no reason thereof, I judge it most unreasonable to imagine, inasmuch as He worketh all things according to the counsel of His will (verse 11), and whatever is done with counsel, hath of necessity some reason why it should be done." ("St. Paul's Epistles," p. 285)

R. W. Dale, in his work on Ephesians, said: "It was the divine purpose that all who are in Christ should be an elect race. . . . The elect are those who are 'in Christ,' and that being in Him they enter into the possession of those eternal blessings which before the foundation of the world it was God's purpose, His decree, to confer upon all Christians. . . .

According to Paul no man is elect except he is 'in Christ.' We are all among the nonelect until we are in Him. But once in Christ we are caught in the currents of the eternal purposes of the divine love; we belong to the elect race. . . . If we consent to receive Christ as the Lord and Giver of life we fall into the line of God's eternal purpose, we are God's elect in Him." (*The Expositor's Library,* "Epistle to the Ephesians," pp. 29-32,41)

Harry Ironside, whose work on Ephesians was quoted earlier, said further on these verses: "There is no such thing taught in the Word of God as predestination to eternal condemnation. If men are lost, they are lost because they do not come to Christ. . . . And so you can settle it for yourself whether you will be among the elect of God or not." (*In The Heavenlies*, p. 29)

In the scholarly *International Critical Commentary* on "Ephesians," T. K. Abbott said: "Here what is chiefly in view is not the fact of 'selection,' but the end for which the choice was made (that we should be, etc.). Oltramare argues from the aorist being used, that the election is an act repeated whenever the call is heard. God, before the creation of the world, formed the plan of saving man (all sinners) in Christ. The condition of faith is implicitly contained. The plan is historically realized under the forms of *klēsis* (calling) and *eklogē* (elect). Every man who by faith accepts the call is *eklektos* (elect)." (p. 6)

On verse 11 this writer is most pronounced: " 'We were chosen as His lot or heritage'. . . is not sufficiently supported, and the idea of 'heritage' is without justification. On the other hand, the interpretation, 'we have obtained *klēros* (lot or heritage)' is unobjectionable in point of language . . . and it would be quite in accordance with analogy that *klērousthai* (assigned portion) should be used in the sense 'to be assigned a portion.'. . . The selection of the word is explained by the Old Testament use of *klēros* (heritage), which made it appropriate for the possession allotted to the Jewish Christians (so

Meyer, Soden, Eadie)." (p. 20)

The last part of verse 11 may puzzle some: "According to the purpose of Him who worketh all things after the counsel of His own will." It may be assumed that the counsel of God's will is sovereign and irresistible, but as has been pointed out, the same expression is used in Luke 7:30 where we read that "the Pharisees and lawyers rejected the counsel of God against themselves."

On this, one writer said: "The word 'counsel' represents not His advice, but His plan or purpose, according to the unvarying usage of the Greek word. By the exercise of their free will they rejected His purpose, thereby depriving themselves of the blessing which He intended them to receive through it. In any scriptural theory of predestination such facts ought to find a place." (H. E. Guillebaud, *Some Moral Difficulties of the Bible,* p. 61)

Again, in concluding this verse, the writer in Ellicott's popular commentary called attention to a scholarly work thus: "Hooker, in a well-known passage (*Ecclesiastical Polity* 1:2), quotes it as excluding the notion of an arbitrary will of God, 'they err, who think that of God's will there is no reason except His will.' " ("Ephesians," p. 19)

2 Thessalonians 2:13—"God hath from the beginning chosen you to salvation."

This verse is often cited as conclusive proof that God's election is to salvation. Such use of this text, however, overlooks certain important facts.

First of all, the word "chosen" in this verse is not the common word for elect or predestinate. Indeed, J. B. Lightfoot said, "The word does not occur elsewhere in the New Testament in this meaning. . . . A rare word in any sense." (*Notes on the Epistles of St. Paul,* p. 119)

Furthermore, in the light of the context we see the

principle set down that unbelievers perish because they "receive not the love of the truth" (verse 10) and "believe not the truth" (verse 12); while the other group are called "brethren" predicated upon "belief of the truth" (verse 13). There is manifest here a most significant parallelism.

Notice next the goal of the choosing or appointment. It is not of the unsaved (or unregenerate) to become believers, but of "brethren beloved" looking forward to a certain aspect of salvation, as the very next verse says: "to the obtaining of the glory of our Lord Jesus Christ." What a wonderful future awaits God's children! Dr. A. T. Robertson said concerning "unto salvation," "The ultimate goal, final salvation." (*Word Pictures in the New Testament,* Vol. IV, p. 54) Alexander Maclaren, quoting this part of verse 13, applied it not to some point in the eternal past, but "We are summoned here and now to a life of purity and righteousness and self-sacrifice." (*Expositions of Holy Scripture,* "2 Thessalonians," p. 259-260)

Some may question all this in the light of the phrase "from the beginning." In the *Cambridge Greek Testament,* G. G. Findlay said: "It is doubtful whether *ap' arkēs* (from the beginning) looks further back than to the time when God's call in the gospel reached the Thessalonians; without some indication in the context, the reader would hardly think here of a *pretemporal* election. The *eklogia* (election) of I 1:4 was associated with the arrival of the gospel at Thessalonica (I 1:5,9). Then, practically and to human view, 'God chose' this people—i.e., took them for His own out of the evil world in which they moved." (p. 189)

We find, generally, that there are two views of "from the beginning," but in the light of the context we note that the viewpoint just given has scholarly support. Fausset, in *Jamieson, Fausset and Brown's Commentary,* said: ". . . other oldest mss. and Vulgate read, 'as first-fruits.' The Thessalonians were among the first converts in Europe (cf., Romans 16:5, 1 Corinthians 16:15). In a more general sense it occurs in James 1:18, Revelation 14:4; so I understand it here including the most restricted sense." (op. cit., p. 398)

The contemporary Greek scholar, F. F. Bruce, while recognizing the two possibilities, in the text of his translation placed as preferred "as firstfruits." (*Expanded Paraphrase of the Epistles of Paul,* p. 61)

A Baptist writer called attention to what the German scholar, B. Weiss, had to say on this: "It is an old error to maintain that according to New Testament teaching, this [appointment for eternal life] is based on an eternal decree of election. This opinion is based on 2 Thessalonians 2:13 where, according to the corrected reading, it is not said that God had selected the readers from the beginning, but that He has chosen them to be first fruits (dedicated to Him)." (B. Weiss, *The Religion of the New Testament,* p. 293)

In Ellicott's *New Testament Commentary for English Readers* it is suggested that "from the beginning" refers to that which goes back to eternity, yet this work says: "It is not an absolute irreversible predestination to a particular state of happiness on which the elect is to enter after death. The 'salvation' is present, begun in this life. . . . If God chose the Thessalonian Christians to salvation by a course of sanctification and belief, one thing, at any rate, is clear: that if any of them should leave that course, and fall into the errors and sins denounced in the foregoing verses, then, in the apostle's mind, they would have forfeited their salvation, in spite of God's choice of them. Consequently, we are forced to one of two theories; either that the man has no free will at all, the moral character of his actions depending as entirely upon God as his final destiny; or else, that the man is free, and that God singles him out to enjoy special opportunities of sanctification and of correct belief, which the man may accept or reject as he pleases. . . . 'Belief of truth' is opposed to 'believing the lie,' of verse 11: acceptation of facts as they are, especially the deep facts of revelation, is always the great means of sanctification in Holy Scripture (John 17:17)." (pp. 158-159)

Pastor Edward Drew wrote on this passage: "The question is what that word 'beginning' means. Evidently it means from the time Paul went there to preach, from the beginning of his preaching there, they believed, and God chose them. Look at the next verse, please (2 Thessalonians 2:14): *Whereunto He called you by our gospel . . .* (Revelation 17:14) . . . *they that are with Him are called, and chosen, and faithful.* Now when is the choosing? After the calling. Paul said, 'I went, and God called you by my gospel.' And the choosing came after the calling. Now that is God's order. In 2 Peter 1:10 you have calling before election. . . . You have here that God's people are called, and when they respond, they are chosen, and then they are the faithful and glorified. So evidently the word 'beginning' in 2 Thessalonians 2:13 refers to the time that Paul entered there and began to preach." (*Studies in the Second Epistle of Paul to the Thessalonians,* No. 16)

1 Peter 1:1-2—"Elect according to the foreknowledge of God the Father."

See above on the general treatment of "Elect" and "Election," and "Foreknowledge."

In the original the word "elect" is in the first verse, and is rendered in both the old English revision and the American 1901 revision as, "to the elect who are sojourners of the Dispersion." Others render it as "chosen" and employ it as an adjective before the ones specified; so Rotherham, Young's *Literal Translation*; Ferrar Fenton, *Twentieth Century New Testament*; Beck's *New Testament in the Language of Today*; and *Good News for Modern Man.*

A. T. Robertson, likewise, set forth this sense, and referring to the *International Critical Commentary* said: "Bigg takes *eklektois* . . . as an adjective describing the next word, 'to elect sojourners.' That is possible and is like *genos eklekton* in 2:9." And Robertson suggested no other alternative. (*Word Pictures in the New Testament,* Vol. VI, pp. 78-79)

Turning to the *International Critical Commentary* itself, we find in one brief paragraph Bigg said: "Elect, in fact, means simply Christian. What the apostle is thinking of is corporate citizenship among the elect people; the individual elements of the new life are faith and obedience." (*A Critical and Exegetical Commentary on the Epistles of St. Peter and St. Jude,* p. 90)

While some hold other views, a number of writers suggest that "according to the foreknowledge of God" (verse 2) points to God's knowledge long ago of those who would exercise the requisite faith. Some years ago Dr. Howard W. Ferrin wrote in *Strengthen Thy Brethren, A Devotional Exposition of the First Epistle of Peter:* "None can know the depth of meaning in these words, but we are of the opinion they mean that from all eternity God has known those who would accept the overtures of mercy. Shall we say that He foresaw there were to be children of faith who would cleave to Christ, and therefore prove themselves to be sons of the faith; and all these He foreknew and predestinated to be conformed to the image of His Son." (p. 14)

Similarly, Dr. L. S. Keyser said: "The apostle even says here the 'elect *according to* the foreknowledge of God,' which shows that God's election is determined by His foreknowledge. Then He could have foreknown those who would humble themselves and accept His grace by simple faith and self-surrender. The fact is, Peter does not give much support to the doctrine of unconditional election, for he says (2 Peter 1:10): 'Wherefore, brethren, give the more diligence to make your calling and election sure; for if ye do these things, ye shall never stumble.' " (*Election and Conversion*, p. 129)

At any rate, as still others have pointed out, taken with the context we see that it all is looking ahead to the future position and blessings of the believer (as indicated earlier, is included in the goal of election). As verse 4 says, "To an inheritance . . . reserved in Heaven for you," and verse 5, "unto salvation ready to be revealed in the last time." How wonderful that God has a sure future planned out for those who become children of His.

Let it be understood that we should not look at just one side of things when more is presented. We must get in view all that Peter says about the matter. In this same chapter the human aspect of the subject is brought out along with the divine. For example, in verse 5 we find that we are "kept by the power of God," the divine side; "through faith," the human side. The latter part should not be neglected. On this verse, Hart, in the *Expositor's Greek Testament,* said: "so long as they have faith (verse 9) they are safe. . . . Without responsive faith God's power is powerless to heal or to guard." (Vol. V, p. 42) Similarly, Fausset, in *Jamieson, Fausset, and Brown's Commentary* said: "Let none flatter himself he is being guarded by the power of God unto salvation, if he be not walking by faith. . . . It is through faith that salvation is both received and kept." (p. 499)

F. B. Meyer had some pointed words on this: "The power of the Holy Ghost works through our faith. God will do all that we can trust Him to do; but He does not pledge Himself to work independently of our faith. When faith is in strong and blessed exercise, there is no limit to its possibilities, because it taps the reservoirs of Omnipotence, and opens the sluice gates, so that all God's power begins to flow into the soul. Our faith is the means of our receptivity. . . . But if our faith be meager and struggling, we cannot expect mighty deliverance. . . . According to your faith, or unbelief, so will it be done to you." (*Tried by Fire, Expositions of the First Epistle of Peter,* p. 26)

Another voice may be heard on this verse (1 Peter 1:5). Alexander Maclaren said: "Many people seem to think that faith is appointed by God as the condition of salvation out of mere arbitrary selection and caprice. Not at all. If God could save you without your faith, He would do it. He does not, because He cannot. Why must I have faith in order that God's power may keep me? Why must you open your window in order to let the fresh air in? Why must you pull up the blind in order to let the light in? Why must you take your medicine or your food if you want to be cured or nourished?. . . Unless I trust God, distrusting myself . . . God cannot pour out upon me His power. There is nothing arbitrary about it. . . . My unbelief can thwart Omnipotence, and hinder Christ's all-loving purpose, just as on earth we read that 'He could there do no mighty works because of their unbelief.' I am sure that there are people here who all their lives long have been thus hampering Omnipotence and neutralizing the love of Christ, and making His sacrifice impotent and His wish to save them vain. Stretch out your hands as this very Peter once did, crying, 'Lord, save, or I perish,' and He will answer. . . . Salvation, here and hereafter, is God's work alone. It cannot be exercised toward a man who has not faith. It will certainly be exercised toward any man who has." (*Expositions of Holy Scripture,* "First Peter," pp. 15-16)

Once more, in 1 Peter 1:9, the sacred writer speaks of full salvation being the outcome "of your faith." "Receiving the end of your faith, even the salvation of your souls."

And in the twenty-second verse, even more strikingly, the writer brings out human agency, "Seeing ye have purified your souls in obeying the truth." To quote again Alexander Maclaren, this time on this twenty-second verse: "The language in the original here implies that there was a given definite moment in the past when these dispersed strangers obeyed, and, by obeying the truth, purified their souls. What was that moment?. . . I would say the moment when they bowed themselves in joyful acceptance of the great Word and put out a firm hand of faith to grasp Jesus Christ. That is obedience; and the moment when a man believes, in the deepest sense of the word, that moment, in the deepest realities of his spirit, he becomes obedient to the will and to the love of his Saviour Lord." (A. Maclaren, *Expositions of Holy Scripture,* "First Peter," p. 80)

Revelation 13:8—"Whose names are not written in the book of life of the Lamb slain from the foundation of the world," and Revelation 17:8—"Whose names were not written in the book of life from the foundation of the world."

Some have thought that these verses show that the names of all the saved have been recorded in the book of life from the foundation of the world. But that is *not* what is said. Note that the statements quoted are negative, and nothing can be established on a negative. It is merely said that the names of the unsaved, the followers of the beast, are not in the book of life. That the names of all the saved have been recorded from away back is nowhere stated. It is similar to the observation that as the saved are said to be predestinated to a glorious future, but the unsaved are never said to be elected to a lost state; so—the other way around—the Word speaks of those whose names are not in the book of life, but it never says that others' names have been recorded there from the beginning of the world.

Revelation 13:8 is sometimes quoted in the Revised Version as showing certain names not having been *written from* the foundation of the world: "whose name hath not been written from the foundation of the world in the book of life of the Lamb that had been slain." However, many scholars contend for the old order which puts the "from the foundation of the world" not with the matter of the names, but with the Lamb slain, as A.V. So, Fausset (in *Jamieson, Fausset and Brown's Commentary*) said: "The Greek order of words favors this translation," and it "is in the Greek more obvious and simple." Dean Alford (*New Testament for English Readers*) went farther and said: it "is far more obvious and natural: and had it not been for the apparent difficulty of the sense thus conveyed, the going so far back as to *is written* for a connection would never have been thought of." Similarly, Dr. A. T. Robertson (*Word Pictures in the New Testament,* Vol. VI, p. 402) said: "Here the most natural use is with *esphagmenou* (slain). At any rate the death of Christ lies in the purpose of God." Again, A. Plummer in *The Pulpit Commentary* declared: "It is natural to connect the words, 'from the foundation of the world,' with 'slain,' and not with 'written' . . . because from 'the foundation of the world' His death has been efficacious for the salvation of men; and because His death 'was foreordained before the foundation of the world,' although manifest only in the last times (1 Peter 1:20)." (p. 333)

Bishop Wordsworth (*Greek Testament With Notes*) pointed out: "His death was foretold in prophecies, even from the beginning of the world . . . and His death had a saving efficacy for all men, even from the beginning." (The same view is taken in *Ellicott's Commentary*; by Craven in *Lange's Commentary*; and by Vincent: *Word Studies in the New Testament*; etc.)

Getting down to the main point involved in these verses, no less an authority than J. B. Lightfoot said: "In the Revelation *the book of life* is a phrase of constant recurrence [references given]. It is clear from the expression 'blotting out of the book' (Revelation 3:5), that the image suggested no idea of absolute predestination." (*St. Paul's Epistle to the Philippians*, p. 159, on Philippians 4:3)

Another noted linguist and New Testament scholar, Archbishop Trench, had this to say on the matter: "The pledge and promise which is here given [Revelation 3:5] . . . has proved not a little perplexing to those followers of Augustine, who will not be content in this mystery of predestination with having *some* Scripture on their side, and leaving the reconciliation of these and those others which are plainly against them, and apparently contradictory to these, for another and a higher state of knowledge; but who would fain make it appear that *all* Scripture is on their side. If this passage had stood by itself, it would not have been hard for them to answer, as indeed they do answer. . . . But, unhappily, beside and behind this passage, there are others not capable of this solution, and principally Exodus 32:32; Psalm 69:28; Revelation 22:19. To what hard shifts they are put in forcing these statements within the limits of their system may be judged by Augustine's comment on the second of these." (*Epistles to the Seven Churches of Asia,* pp. 222-223)

On a similar text (Philippians 4:3) Alexander Maclaren very pointedly declared: "Remember that names can be blotted out of the book. The metaphor has often been pressed into the service of a doctrine of unconditional and irreversible predestination. But rightly looked at, it points in the opposite direction. Remember Moses' agonized cry, 'Blot me out of Thy book'; and the divine answer, 'Him that sinneth against Me, his name will I blot out of My book.' And remember that it is only to 'him that overcometh' that the promise is made, 'I will not blot him out.' We are made partakers of Christ if we 'hold fast the beginning of our confidence firm unto the end.'

"Remember that it depends upon ourselves whether our names are there or not. John Bunyan describes the armed man who came up to the table, where the man with the inkhorn was seated, and said: 'Set down my name.' And you and I may do that. If we cast ourselves on Jesus Christ and yield our wills to be guided by Him, and give our lives for His service, then He will write our names in His book." (*Expositions of Holy Scripture,* Philippians, pp. 20-21)

Relating verses as these to practical aspects of the gospel, William E. Biederwolf said, "When I took Christ for myself and let His atoning work stand for me, my name was transferred from 'the books' (Revelation 20:12) and written over on 'the book of life,' and the old record on 'the books' was blotted out." (*Later Evangelistic Sermons,* p. 91)

Somewhat similarly, Lehman Strauss brought out human

responsibility here: "Each individual must determine for himself whether or not his name remains in the book of life. This is just as true of the Jew as it is of the Gentile (Daniel 12:1).... What each of us does with Christ now will be the determining factor in the day of judgment." (*The Book of the Revelation,* p. 120)

Apropos of this, Dr. William Evans said: "Has it ever impressed you as strange that God has no 'book of death'? At least there is no record in the Scripture anywhere of such a book.... Is it not true that it is man by his own willful neglect who commits spiritual suicide? God's will and desire for all men is that they should be saved (1 Timothy 2:4). Men themselves are the guilty cause why they are blotted out of the book of life, or perhaps better, why their names are not written in that book." (*Christ's Last Message to His Church,* p. 175)

APPENDIX A

SPURGEON ON THE EXTENT OF THE ATONEMENT

Here again words have been loosely spoken and assertions have been bandied about. Discussion on the point can become a bit academic. A little reflection will show that it is all a matter of how the terms employed are to be understood. If by Christ dying for the whole world (unlimited atonement) we are to understand that every member of the human race will ultimately be saved, of course we reject that suggestion; that is universalism, wholly repudiated by orthodox Bible believers. But if by atonement for all we mean that Christ's death is potentially adequate for every man, that appears to be the teaching of Scripture* and is held to by a host of men true to the faith. As the old saying has it, the atonement is sufficient for all, efficient only for those who believe. Christ died only for the elect in the sense that those only will ultimately be in Heaven, the full beneficiaries of His atonement. But He also died for all those who finally will be in hell, insofar as His death would have been adequate for them had they believed.

But it is best to let Spurgeon speak for himself here. And that he did in strong words: "I know there are some who think it necessary to their system of theology to limit the merit of the blood of Jesus: if my theological system needed such limitation, I would cast it to the winds. I cannot, I dare

*The Scriptures usually cited as showing that the atonement was for all men are: 1 John 2:2; 1 Timothy 2:3-4,6; Hebrews 2:9; 1 Corinthians 15:22; John 1:29; 2 Peter 2:1; Isaiah 53:6; 2 Corinthians 5:14-15,19.

not, allow the thought to find a lodging in my mind, it seems so near akin to blasphemy. In Christ's finished work I see an ocean of merit; my plummet finds no bottom, my eye discerns no shore. There must be sufficient efficacy in the blood of Christ, if God had so willed it, to have saved not only all the world, but all in ten thousand worlds, had they transgressed their Master's law. Once admit infinity into the matter and limit is out of the question. Having a divine Person for an offering, it is not consistent to conceive of limited value; bound and measure are terms inapplicable to the divine sacrifice. The intent of the divine purpose fixes the application of the infinite offering, but does not change it into a finite work." (*Spurgeon's Autobiography*, Vol. I, p. 174)

Spurgeon quite evidently rejected on the one hand the idea that the sins of the impenitent have automatically been removed, yet on the other hand he decried, as we have pointed out, an attempt to change "have all men to be saved" (1 Timothy 2:4) into "some men," or into "not have all men" to be saved.

APPENDIX B

DR. BIEDERWOLF'S EXCERPT FROM KINSLEY ON GOD'S FOREKNOWLEDGE

In a previously quoted book by Dr. William E. Biederwolf we find an extended statement on "God's perfect foreknowledge." It is taken from a book by W. W. Kinsley with the title "*Science and Prayer*" which was once one of the required books for the Chautauqua Literary and Scientific Circle. We present it here just as Dr. Biederwolf gave it, including an introductory and concluding paragraph by Dr. Biederwolf which intimated his agreement with the position taken.

"A controversion of God's perfect foreknowledge does not set well with most of us, regardless of our denominational bias. The fear, however, of any belittling conception of God, its advocates would overcome by showing what the theory of such foreknowledge really involves, leaving us to decide which is the greater injustice, if any, to the all-perfect character of God.

"The following from the work *Science and Prayer* will help us to an appreciation, if so be such is possible, of the position assumed by the advocates of the limited knowledge theory. The author [W. W. Kinsley] says: 'No petitioner can plead with any genuine unction unless he believes that he can actually effect some change in the purposes existing in the divine mind at the time his prayer is offered. . . . If God foreknows everything that will ever come to pass, all His own mental states must necessarily be included in that foreknowledge. A moment's reflection will convince us that otherwise there is not a single present intention or plan but what is exposed to the possibility of modification. If a single thought or emotion is ever going to spring up in God's mind unanticipated, God Himself must be as ignorant as we as to what part of His vast plan it will pertain. And so, if we would logically defend a belief in the all-comprehensiveness of God's foreknowledge, we must affirm that not a single new idea can arise in His mind—not a single new emotion be felt—and that if He is thus limited now, He must have been equally so at every moment in all the eternal past, and must be through all the years to come; for if there ever has been, or ever will be, a moment when a new thought can thus come, then during all the time preceding that moment the foreknowledge was incomplete. Where does this lead? In what sort of an intellectual or emotional condition does this irrefragable logic compel us to assert God to be continually? Unquestionably that of perfect stagnation. No thought processes can be carried on under such conditions—no succession of ideas, no change of mental state; but God must have been and must still be imprisoned in a hopelessly dead calm. . . . When, then, did He form His plans for creation? Under this supposition there never could have been a time when He began to think about them. . . . If God has had no thought succession, He can have had no feelings; His emotional state having ever necessarily been that of unbroken placidity—of absolute apathy, His heart throbless as a stone. He could experience no change of feeling, for that would involve thought-succession. From all the sources of joy or sorrow of which we can conceive, He would be utterly debarred—from pleasurable or painful memories, from hopes and forebodings, from social sympathies, from emotions that accompany changes, contrasts, surprises, from the glow of activity, even from the delights and griefs of contemplation; for they all involve thought-movement. Therefore, under this supposition God can have no emotional activity, for He would have no thought-activity for its background. Thoughts must, of course, come and go, or the heart lies dead. Such are the absurdities in which we become hopelessly entangled the moment we attempt to defend the doctrine of God's perfect foreknowledge.' "

Dr. Biederwolf immediately followed these words with this statement: "No Christian scholar would for one second espouse or teach a doctrine of which he has the least suspicion that it is in any sense derogatory to God. For the writer it is impossible to conceive of God's all-comprehending foreknowledge and absolute predestination without including His mental states, for blindly and irrationally He certainly does not act, and because this is true, the conclusions of the above author, some seem to think, are well nigh irresistible." (*How Can God Answer Prayer?*, third edition, pp. 115-118)

APPENDIX C

PINK ON HUMAN RESPONSIBILITY

There are those who take the words of Ephesians 2:1 to mean that since an unregenerate sinner is 'dead in trespasses and sins' he cannot *do* anything in relation to personal salvation. After all, a dead person cannot even sit up! A. W. Pink's view on this will interest the reader.

A.W. Pink (1886-1952) is famous for his calvinistic book *The Sovereignty Of God* which he wrote in 1921. The British edition, published by *The Banner of Truth Trust* in 1961 has sold more than 160,000 copies world-wide and has converted many to a calvinistic viewpoint. Few people know, however, that *Banner of Truth* omitted three chapters from Pink's original book, and specifically edited out his teaching that God has no love for any other than the elect. *Banner of Truth* maintains that Pink modified his more extreme calvinistic reasonings over the years, thus justifying their alterations. The chapters omitted were: ch. 5 'The Sovereignty of God in Reprobation'; ch. 8 'God's Sovereignty and Human Responsibility'; and ch. 11 'Difficulties and Objections'. In these chapters Pink strongly taught that God, by an eternal immutable decree, ordained that certain of Adam's descendants [the majority] should be damned in hell and that therefore God never purposed to give them faith.

Pink edited and privately published a magazine called *Studies in the Scriptures* from 1922-1953. As early as 1927 there was evidence that he had indeed changed his views on human responsibility and had begun to regret some of his earlier more extreme statements. Although he remained a Calvinist to the end, those who scrutinise Pink's writings have noted that his thoughts did alter very decidedly on matters relative to sovereignty and human freedom.

Regarding the 'dead' state of the sinner, Pink stated in 1927: 'There are some who say, the unregenerate are dead, and *that* ends the matter — they *cannot* have any responsibility. But this is manifestly erroneous . . . The Hyper-Calvinist is fond of asking, "Would any sensible man go to the cemetery and bid those in the graves to come forth! Why, then, ask anyone who is dead in sins to come to Christ, when he is equally incapable of responding?" Such a question only betrays the ignorance of the one who puts it. A corpse in the cemetery is no suitable analogy of the natural man. A corpse in the cemetery is incapable of performing evil! A corpse cannot "despise and reject" Christ (*Isa* 53:3), cannot "resist the Holy Spirit" (*Acts* 7:51), cannot disobey the gospel (2 *Thess* 1:8); but the natural man can and does do these things!" (*Studies In The Scriptures*, 1927, pp. 260-1).

Maintaining a balance between God's sovereignty and human responsibility is essential for all Bible students. Indeed, the scriptures abound with examples of such balance. Take, for instance, the gospel incident of the woman with the issue of blood and Jairus's daughter. The former came of her own will to Christ and was healed when she grasped the hem of His garment; the latter was dead and only when Christ came to her and took her by the hand was it possible for her to be restored to life (Mark 5:22-43). Of humanity it is true to state; no free will, no responsibility: of deity, no sovereignty, no God.

APPENDIX D

AN ANSWER TO JOHN OWEN

One of the greatest champions of the Calvinistic cause, if not *the* greatest, was John Owen, the 'Calvin of England' (1616-83). It is often claimed that, after 300 years, his logical arguments for 'five point' Calvinism have still not been answered. The fact is they have been answered many times and from many quarters.

One of Owen's most quoted and, at first sight, extremely potent and logical arguments was answered by Robert P. Lightner Th.D. in his book *The Death Christ Died, A Case For Unlimited Atonement* (Regular Baptist Press, 1967), now published by Kregel Publications. The following quotation from pages 100-1 of this book contains both Owen's argument and Lightner's answer:

"In a refutation of Arminianism, John Owen put the question bluntly: 'God imposed his wrath due unto, and Christ underwent the pains of hell for, either all the sins of all men, or all the sins of some men, or some sins of all men. If the last, some sins of all men, then have all men some sins to answer for, and so shall no man be saved. If the second, that is it which we affirm, that Christ in their stead and room suffered for all the sins of all the elect in the world. If the first, why, then are not all freed from the punishment of all their sins? You will say "Because of their unbelief; they will not believe." But this unbelief, is it a sin or not? If not, why should they be punished for it? If it be, then Christ underwent the punishment due to it, or not. If so, then why must that hinder them more than their other sins for which he died from partaking of the fruit of his death? If he did not, then did he not die for all their sins.'

"Owen seems here to present the case as an either-or

proposition. Either Christ died for the sin of unbelief and all for whom He died are saved, or He did not and no one is saved. In answer to this argument, the sin of unbelief is always associated with the completed work of Christ and thus assumes a specific quality and is treated in a particular way in Scripture. Owen's argument may be reversed and the problem stated this way: If Christ's death apart from any other considerations included the sin of unbelief, why does God ask men to believe since they would not be lost for not believing? A request from God for faith to apply the benefits of the cross becomes redundant. Why should God ask men to believe if that is not the sole condition of salvation? Or why does it matter whether they believe or not if their rejection and unbelief in Christ as Saviour has been paid for? Why ask men to exercise faith for salvation if they are saved already by virtue of election and the atonement? Limited redemptionists not only remove the voluntariness from faith but they also make it an unnecessary routine, the refusal of which Christ atoned for and the exercise of which cannot be avoided. This argument of Owen's and all limited redemptionists only serves to prove what we have sought to establish earlier, namely, that limited redemptionists believe the death of Christ saves. Faith, in actuality, becomes a rather unnecessary thing, and salvation has no condition whatsoever.

"The necessity of faith for salvation serves to demonstrate the provisional aspect of atonement. The sin of unbelief is a problem for the limited redemptionists, for if his view be carried through consistently it would mean the elect would not even be born in sin and thus would not be subject to the wrath and condemnation of God before they believe, nor would they ever need to be forgiven and declared righteous before God since that has already been done at the cross. Looking at this problem from the standpoint of those for whom Christ did not die, it could be said that they would not be lost for rejecting Christ as Saviour since, according to the limited view, Christ is not offered to them nor has He died for them; therefore, He could not be rejected by them."

Quoted with permission of Regular Baptist Press, Schaumburg, Illinois, U.S.A.

APPENDIX E

GOD'S WILLINGNESS and MAN'S UNWILLINGNESS

This is a long appendix, but for the patient reader it will prove to be a solid exposition of the truth that a sovereign God often desires things that never actually come to pass. This is a problem for Calvinism that will not go away.

Introduction

In no uncertain terms the Bible declares that God is a sovereign God who "worketh all things after the council of His own will" and who has "done whatsoever He hath pleased" (Eph. 1:11; Ps. 115:3). We must, however, be careful to distinguish between two kinds of *decrees* (which have to do with the sovereign outworking of God's eternal plan). There are *efficacious* decrees whereby God purposes to accomplish something directly by Himself (examples of this would be the creation of the world, the virgin birth, etc.). Man has nothing to do with these things. God's direct will and activity brings them about. There are also *permissive* decrees whereby God decides to accomplish His overall purpose of bringing glory to Himself by allowing His creatures to perform in certain ways. He even allows His creatures to act in a way that is contrary to the desire and wish of the Creator (we call this *sin*). For example, God did not wish Adam to sin as indicated by His command to the contrary (Gen. 2:16-17), but God allowed Adam to sin and this terrible sin and fall was part of God's overall plan whereby He would ultimately bring glory to Himself.

Extreme Calvinists seem to have difficulty in understanding

how a sovereign God can "desire" something that will never come to pass. They believe that whatever God desires must come to pass. If God desires to save certain men, then these must be saved. If Christ loved the world, then the world must be saved. If Christ died for all men, then all men must be saved. This is how they would reason. Of course, they believe that Christ died only for the elect, and that everyone who Christ died for (that is, the elect) will be saved. As one writer has said in light of 1 Timothy 2:4: "What God *desires* that He will do" (thus he believes that the "all men" in this verse refers only to the elect). They feel that if God wants men to repent, then they will repent (God will work in their hearts and bring about repentance).

They can't seem to understand how God could love someone and not save that person. For example, the Scripture says that Christ loved the rich young ruler (Mark 10:21), a man who "went away" and as far as we know never followed Christ. A.W. Pink cannot believe that Christ would love a man who would never be saved. He said, "We fully believe that he was one of God's elect, and was 'saved' sometime after his interview with the Lord." This is what Pink said, but not the Scripture.

If God is willing, then the extreme Calvinist believes that man must be willing also, because God makes him so. If man is unwilling, then it must be because God was unwilling to make the person willing. The Scripture, however, teaches that even though God is willing, He often *allows men to have their own way* and *go their own way according to the stubbornness of their own self-hardened hearts*. God was willing, but they were not. God would, but they would not!

Thus our purpose in this study is to examine certain key words (especially in the Old Testament) which demonstrate that God's compassion and desire and invitation does indeed reach out to all men, even to those who refuse to repent and believe and come to Him. We shall see the wonderful willingness of God in sharp contrast to the stubborn unwillingness of man. We will gain a better appreciation for our Lord's words in Matthew 23:37 which cannot be fully understood apart from certain Old Testament passages that we shall study. May the Lord open our eyes to these truths!

The Hebrew Verb אָבָה

This verb means "*to be willing*, to consent, to desire, to wish." It is an interesting verb because it is always used with a negative particle except for two places (Isa. 1:19 and Job 39:9). Thus, with the negative it means "to be unwilling, to refuse." For example, in Exodus 10:27 it is used of Pharoah's stubborn refusal to let the children of Israel go ("he would not", he refused!). This word is also illustrated in 2 Samuel 23:16 where David refused to drink the water ("he would not") even though he was terribly thirsty. This word is also used in Isaiah 42:24 (Israel's refusal to walk in God's ways) and in Ezekiel 3:7 (used twice) and 20:8 (Israel's refusal to listen to God). The following pasages which contain this verb especially relate to our study:

1) Psalm 81:11—"But my people would not hearken to my voice, and Israel *would have none* of me." God wanted them to open their mouth wide (v.10). God wanted to bless them and fill them (v.10). God earnestly desired that they should hearken unto Him and walk in His ways (how could God's willingness and desire be stated any clearer than in verse 13?) God was willing! God would have done so much for them (verses 14-16), but they *would not*. They refused! God had a heart for them; they had no heart for God.

2) Proverbs 1:25,30—"But ye have set at nought all my counsel, and *would have none* of my reproof . . . They *would have none* of my counsel; they despised all my reproof." Is God willing that men should love simplicity and hate knowledge (v.22), Wisdom cries out (v.20) and invites men (v.23) and promises great things to those who come to her (v.23). God was willing; man was unwiling (v. 25, 30).

3) Isaiah 28:12—"This is the rest by which ye may cause the weary to rest, and this is the refreshing; yet they *would not*

hear." God graciously offered rest (compare Matthew 11:28) and refreshment, but they refused (Compare Jer. 6:16). God was willing to give them rest but they were unwilling to receive it.

4) Isaiah 30:15—"For thus saith the Lord GOD, the Holy One of Israel: In returning and rest shall ye be saved; in quietness and in confidence shall be your strength: and ye *would not*." God graciously offered rest and deliverence, but the rebellious ones (v.1,9) refused. They said NO (v.16) to God's offer.

5) Isaiah 1: 19—"If ye be *willing* and obedient, ye shall eat the good of the land." This is one of those rare places where the verb is used without the negative. God's desire was that they would be clean (v.16). God wanted them to learn to do well (v.17). God was willing to reason with them and to offer them the forgiveness of sins (v.18). God was willing. Would they be willing (v.19) or would they refuse (v.20)?

The Hebrew Verb מָאֵן

This verb means the opposite to the last verb. It means "to refuse, to be unwilling, to refuse with a resolved mind." Thus it means the very same thing as AAA with the negative. Pharaoh is a good illustration of this verb also. In Exodus 7:14 he refused to let the people go. Let us now examine some of the passages where this verb is used.

1) Jeremiah 5:3—"O Lord, are not thine eyes upon the truth? Thou hast stricken them, but they have not grieved; thou hast consumed them, but they have *refused* to receive correction. They have made their faces harder than a rock; they have *refused* to return." God wanted Israel to return to Himself (Jer. 4:1) but they refused! God was willing, they were not.

2) Jeremiah 11:10—"They are turned back to the iniquities of their forefathers, who *refused* to hear my words." God earnestly protested to their fathers (v.7) because He wanted

them to obey His voice (v.7), but they refused (v.8). God wanted them to obey, He allowed them to walk in the imagination of their evil heart (v.8).

3) 1 Samuel 8:19—"Nevertheless, the people *refused* to obey the voice of Samuel; and they said, Nay, but we will have a king over us." God was willing to be their king and the Lord was grieved that they had rejected Him (v.7).

4) Nehemiah 9:16-17—"But they and our fathers dealt proudly, and hardened their necks, and hearkened not to thy commandments, and *refused* to obey." God was ready, willing and eager to pardon and to be merciful and to hold back His anger (v.17), but the people who lived in the days of Moses refused to obey.

5) Proverbs 1:24—"Because I called and ye *refused*; I have stretched out my hand, and no man regarded." God (personified by wisdom, v.20) called but man refused! God was willing to pour out His spirit unto them and make known His words to them, but they were unwilling (verses 23-24). God stretched out His hand (v.24) but they could not care less.

6) Isaiah 1:20—"But if ye *refuse* and rebel, ye shall be devoured with the sword." God was willing and able to PARDON and WASH His people from their sins (verses 16,18). He was willing to pour out His blessing and give them the good of the land (v.19). God was willing, were they?

7) Zechariah 7:11—"But they *refused* to hearken, and pulled away the shoulder, and stopped their ears, that they should not hear." God's will and desire was clearly revealed in His commands. He wanted them to turn from their evil ways (verses 9-10), but they refused to hearken. Their hearts were as hard as stone (v.12).

8) Jeremiah 13:10—"This evil people, who *refuse* to hear my words, who walk in the imagination of their heart, and walk after other gods, to serve them, and to worship them, shall even be like this belt, which is good for nothing." God wanted the whole house of Israel and Judah to be unto Him

for a people and for a name and for a praise and for a glory (v.11). This was His desire, but THEY WOULD NOT HEAR (v.11). THEY REFUSED TO HEAR (v.10).

The Hebrew Verb בָּחַר

This is the common Hebrew verb which means *to choose*, to select, to elect." This word has been made famous by Joshua in Joshua 24:15: "*choose* ye this day whom ye will serve." Let us now consider some of the other passages that use this word:

1) Deuteronomy 30:19—"I have set before you life and death, blessing and cursing; therefore, *choose* life, that both thou and thy seed may live." A choice must be made between life and death, good and evil (v.15). God wanted men to live and be blessed by loving Him and keeping His commandments (v.16). God, through Moses, warns them about making the wrong choice (verses 17-18). Finally Moses said, CHOOSE LIFE (v.19). Doubtless Moses was reflecting the desire of the living God that He might be their choice.
2) Proverbs 1:29—"Because they hated knowledge, and did not *choose* the fear of the Lord." God was willing (verses 20-23) but man was not (verses 24-25; 29-30).
3) Isaiah 65:12—"When I called, ye did not answer; when I spoke, ye did not hear, but did evil before mine eyes, and did *choose* that in which I delighted not." God was not delighted by their choice! It's obvious that their choice did not please the Lord. It was not God's wish or desire that they should choose in such a way. Notice God's gracious appeal to these people. He "called" (v.12). He "spread out His hands" (v.2). He was willing, but they were not.
4) Isaiah 66:3-4—"Yea, they have *chosen* their own ways and their soul delighteth in their abominations . . . when I called, none did answer; when I spoke, they did hear; but they did evil before mine eyes, and *chose* that in which I delighted not." God allowed these people to go their own sinful ways. The people made a choice and the people were

delighted in the choice they made! God, however, was not delighted in their choice. He was grieved. God wanted the people to chose His ways not their own ways. Their choice was contrary to God's desire.

Hebrew Verbs meaning to Stretch Out the Hands

God's willingness is seen by the way He earnestly and urgently calls to His people and pleads with them and entreats them. How can the Bible writers describe this divine entreaty in terms that we can understand? One of the ways is by picturing God stretching forth His hands as He invites and urges His people to come unto Himself. In Proverbs 1:24 the verb נָטָה is used meaning "to stretch or extend the hand." In Isaiah 65:2 the verb פָּרַשׂ is used with a similar meaning ("to spread out or extend the hands"). Consider the following passages:

1) Proverbs 1:24—"Because I have called, and ye refused; I have *stretched out my hand*, and no man regarded." Here we have wisdom making her wonderful appeal and invitation which man rejects.
2) Isaiah 65:2—"I have *spread out my hands* all the day unto a rebellious people, that walketh in a way that was not good, after their own thoughts." Notice that God was not pleased in the way that they were walking. God stretched out His hands and wanted to draw them unto Himself, but they wanted to go their own way. And God allowed it to be so! God let them have what they wanted even though it was not what He wanted. This verse is quoted by the Apostle Paul in Romans 10:21:
3) Romans 10:21—"But to Israel He saith, All day long I have stretched forth my hands unto a disobedient and gainsaying people." The word "gainsaying" means *rebellious,* contrary, refusing to have anything to do with God." What words could better express God's tender invitation to sinful men as He extends wide His arms. As Hodge remarks: "God has extended wide His arms, and urged men frequently and

long to return to His love." What yearning, what love, what pleading, what patience! As Barnes has said, "This denotes an attitude of entreaty, a *willingness* and *earnest desire* to receive them to favour, to invite and entreat." "The arms outstretched all the day long are the symbol of that incessant pleading love which Israel through all its history has consistently despised" (*Expositor's Greek New Testament*). God was so willing; man was so rebellious!

The New Testament Verb θελω

This common verb means "to wish, desire, be willing, take delight, have pleasure." In the Septuagint it is used frequently and often it corresponds to some of the Hebrew verbs we have already studied. For example, it occurs in Isaiah 1:19-20; Isaiah 28:12; Jeremiah 5:3; 8:5; Ezekiel 3:7; 18:23, 32. Let us now a few New Testament examples of the usage of this word:

1) Matthew 23:37—"Oh Jerusalem, Jerusalem, thou that killest the prophets, and stonest them who are sent unto thee, how often would I have gathered thy children together, even as a hen gathereth her chickens under her wings, and *ye would not*." The verb is used twice in this verse. Jesus was saying: "I would . . . ye would not." "I was willing . . . you were not willing!" God was willing to gather these murderers unto Himself but they were not willing! God wanted to gather them, but they did not want to be gathered! We will say more about this verse later.
2) Luke 13:34—parallel to Matthew 23:37.
3) John 5:40—"And ye *will not* come to Me, that ye may have life." Or "And ye do not desire to come to Me, that ye may have life." Again we see man's wicked refusal to come to the living God. Is God willing that men should come? Let's see:
4) 1 Timothy 2:4—"who *will have* (desires) all men to be saved, and to come unto the knowledge of the truth." This is God's desire for all men. God is willing (1 Tim. 2:4) but man is unwilling (John 5:40).

Note: This verb is often used in relationship to God's will for the believer (1 Thess. 4:3; 5:18; Eph. 5:17-18; etc.). God's will and desire for every believer is that we should be holy, constantly filled with the Spirit and constantly filled with thanksgiving. Yet often we fall short of these things and our God is grieved. God is willing to fill us with Himself, but often we hinder and quench this (compare Psalm 81:10).

The Hebrew Verb חָפֵץ

This verb means "to delight in, take pleasure in." Here are some of the places it is used:

1) Isaiah 65:12—"When I called, ye did not answer; when I spoke, ye did not hear, but did evil before mine eyes, and did choose that in which *I delighted not*." God was not pleased by their choice. He wanted them to choose differently.
2) Isaiah 66:4—"When I called, none did answer; when I spoke, they did not hear; but they did evil before mine eyes, and chose that in which *I delighted not*." God is not delighted when men choose their own ways (v.3) but He allows them to make such a tragic choice. God desires something else, but often He gives men up to their own desires.
3) Ezekiel 18:23—"Have I any *pleasure* at all that the wicked should die? saith the Lord GOD, and not that he should return from his ways, and live?" God is not delighted when men continue in their wicked ways. God is delighted and pleased when the wicked turn from their wicked ways. God's will and wish for every wicked person is this: Turn from your wicked ways and live!
4) Ezekiel 18:32—"For I have no pleasure in the death of him that dieth, saith the Lord GOD; wherefore, turn yourselves, and live." In this verse God answers the question raised in verse 23. God is not willing that sinners should continue in their sin. God is willing that they should turn in the direction of the living God. Question for the extreme Calvinists: if God has no pleasure in the death of the wicked, then why do the wicked die?

5) Ezekiel 33:11—"Say unto them, As I live, saith the Lord GOD, I have no pleasure in the death of the wicked, but that the wicked turn from his way and live; turn ye, turn from your wicked ways; for why will ye die, O house of Israel?" Nothing could be more clear. God desires that the wicked should turn from their evil ways. God pleads with these sinners and urges them to repent and be converted. "Why will ye die, O house of Israel?" Certainly not because God wanted you to die!

The Hebrew Verb שָׁכַם

This interesting verb means "to rise up early in the morning." Thus it came to mean figuratively "speaking early and often, to speak earnestly, eagerly and urgently, to urge earnestly. Let us allow the following verses speak for themselves:

1) 2 Chronicles 36:15-16—"And the LORD God of their fathers sent to them messengers, *rising up early* and sending, because he had compassion on his people, and on his dwelling place. But they mocked the messengers of God, and despised his words."
2) Jeremiah 7:13—"I spake unto you, *rising up early* and speaking, but ye heard not; and I called you, but ye answered not."
3) Jeremiah 7:25-26—"Since the day that your fathers came forth out of the land of Egypt unto this day I have even sent unto you all my servants, the prophets, daily *rising up early* and sending them; yet they hearkened not unto me, nor inclined their ear, but hardened their neck."
4) Jeremiah 11:7-8—"For I earnestly protested unto your fathers in the day that I brought them up out of the land of Egypt, even unto this day, *rising early* and protesting, saying, Obey my voice. Yet they obeyed not, nor inclined their ear, but walked every one in the imagination of their evil heart."
5) Jeremiah 25:3-4—"I have spoken unto you, *rising early* and

speaking, but ye have not hearkened. And the LORD hath sent unto you all his servants, the prophets, *rising early* and sending them, but ye have not hearkened, nor inclined your ear to hear" (see also verse 5).

6) Jeremiah 26:4-5—"If ye will not hearken to me, to walk in my law, which I have set before you, to hearken to the words of my servants, the prophets, whom I sent unto you, both *rising up early* and sending them, but ye have not hearkened..."

7) Jeremiah 29:19—"Because they have not hearkened to my words, saith the LORD, which I sent unto them by my servants, the prophets, *rising up early* and sending them; but ye would not hear, saith the LORD."

8) Jeremiah 32:33—"And they have turned unto me the back, and not the face; though I have taught them, *rising up early* and teaching them, yet they have not hearkened to receive instruction."

9) Jeremiah 35:14-15—"I have spoken to you, *rising early* and speaking, but ye hearkened not unto me. I have sent also unto you all my servants, the prophets, *rising up early* and sending them, saying, Return now every man from his evil way, and amend your doings...but ye have not inclined your ear, nor hearkened unto me."

10) Jeremiah 44:4-5—"I sent unto you all my servants, the prophets, *rising early* and sending them, saying, Oh, do not this abominable thing that I hate. But they hearkened not, nor inclined their ear to turn from their wickedness."

(see also Neh. 9:29-30 and Zech. 1:4 where this word is not used but the same idea is there)

Jeremiah is known as the weeping prophet, but his tears were but a mere reflection of a grieved and weeping God. When this God became a man these tears could again be seen as He wept over Jerusalem (Matthew 23:37; compare Luke 19:41) and said, "*HOW OFTEN* would I have gathered you." These words can only be understood in light of the verses cited above. "How often have I sent my prophets unto you, *rising up early*! How often have I stretched forth my hands unto this rebellious people!

How often have I pleaded and entreated and invited! How often have I called unto you and spoken unto you! How often have I offered you REST and REFRESHMENT! How often would I have filled your mouth if you had but opened it! How often would I have reasoned together with you about your sins! Oh Israel, WHY WILL YOU DIE?? Why do you choose the way that I do not delight in? Why do you go your own way? HOW OFTEN WAS I WILLING TO GATHER YOU UNTO MYSELF BUT YE WERE NOT WILLING!"

I trust that this study has taught something about the terrible depravity of man and the compassionate and tender heart of the Saviour who desires all men to be saved and who has no pleasure in the death of the wicked!

APPENDIX F

A.W. TOZER ON SOVEREIGNTY AND FREE WILL

As most of our readers will know A.W. Tozer (1897-1963) was a prolific author and speaker. He majored on the attributes of God in his life time, devoting much time to speaking and writing on this subject.

On God's sovereignty Tozer often set forth the following profoundly simple explanation; "God's sovereignty and man's free will. That's the toughest problem in theology, I think, tougher than the incarnation . . . You can fall off either end of a log, brother. You don't have to pick one end, you can fall off either end; and, in my opinion, the Calvinist fell off one end, and the Arminians off the other end . . . How do I explain the sovereignty of God and the free will of man? Well, you see, God's sovereignty is God's absolute freedom to do whatever He ordains to do...God created man in His own image, and in His sovereign and absolute freedom He ordained that man was to have a limited amount of freedom; and that was God's sovereign decree; that man should have some freedom. So, when man exercises his freedom, he is fulfilling the sovereignty of God, not cancelling it out." *The Sovereignty Of God* (Audio tape) A.W. Tozer, Camp Hill, Christian Publications, Copyright 1997.

APPENDIX G

SOME LITTLE KNOWN STATEMENTS OF JOHN CALVIN

John Calvin (1509-1564) would be looked upon as an Arminian by some modern day hyper-Calvinists given some of the statements he made in his works. These teachings are not widely known, but they prove that Calvin, albeit inconsistently, actually taught on occasions, that Christ did indeed die for all men.

Mark 14v24: This is my blood of the new testament, which is shed for many. "By the word many He means *not a part of the world only, but the whole human race*; for He contrasts many with one; as if he had said, that He will not be the redeemer of one man only, but will die in order to deliver many from the condemnation of the curse...Therefore, when we approach to the holy table, let us not only remember in general *that the world has been redeemed by the blood of Christ*, but let every one consider for himself that his own sins have been expiated." John Calvin, *Calvin's Commentaries,* Vol. 7, p. 508, Grang Rapids, Associated Publishers and Authors Inc., n.d. (emphasis ours).

Romans 5v18: Therefore as by the offence of one judgment came upon all men to condemnaton; even so by the righteousness of one the free gift came upon all men unto justification of life.

"He makes this favour common to all, because it is propounded to all, and not because it is in reality extended to all; for though *Christ suffered for the sins of the whole world*, and is offered through God's benignity indiscriminately to all, yet all do not receive Him." John Calvin, *op. cit.,* Vol. 11, p. 1401 (emphasis ours).

1 John 2v2: And He is the propitiation for our sins: and not for ours only, but also for the sins of the whole world.

"Here a question may be raised, how have the sins of the whole world been expiated? I pass by the dotages of the fanatics, who under this pretence extend salvation to all the reprobate and therefore to Satan himself. Such a monstrous thing deserves no refutation. Those who seek to avoid this absurdity have said that *Christ suffered sufficiently for the whole world,* but efficiently only for the elect. This solution has commonly prevailed in the schools. Though then *I allow that what has been said is true*, yet I deny it is suitable to this passage." John Calvin, *op. cit.*, Vol. 12, p. 2505 (emphasis ours).

John Calvin's Last Will and Testament, April 24th 1564

"I testify also and declare, that I suppliantly beg of Him, that He may be pleased so to wash and purify me *in the blood which my sovereign redeemer has shed for the sins of the human race*, that under His shadow I may be able to stand at the judgement seat." Quoted from Philip Schaff, *History Of The Christian Church*, Vol. 8, p. 829, Grand Rapids: Eerdmans, 1910 (emphasis ours).

BIBLIOGRAPHY

Works Quoted In This Book

Abbott, T. K. *A Critical and Exegetical Commentary on the Epistle to the Ephesians, The International Critical Commentary*. Edinburgh: T. & T. Clark, 1897.

Alford, Henry. *The New Testament for English Readers.* 4 vols. London, Oxford, and Cambridge: Rivingtons, 1872.

Anderson, Sir Robert. *The Gospel and its Ministry.* 13th ed. rev. Glasgow: Pickering & Inglis, n. d.

Barry, Alfred. *See:* Ellicott, C. J.

Baxter, J. Sidlow. *Explore the Book.* vol. VI, Acts to Revelation. London: Marshall, Morgan & Scott, 1955.

Bertram, R. A., editor. *A Homiletic Encyclopaedia.* 10th ed. New York: Funk & Wagnalls, 1889.

The Biblical Faith of Baptists. vol. I. Detroit: Fundamental Baptist Congress of North America, 1964.

Biederwolf, William Edward. *Evangelistic Sermons, Doctrinal Series.* Chicago: Glad Tidings Publ. Co., n. d.

———. *How Can God Answer Prayer?* 3d ed. Grand Rapids: Wm. B. Eerdmans, n. d.

———. *Later Evangelistic Sermons.* Chicago: Bible Institute Colportage Ass'n, 1925.

Bigg, Charles. *A Critical and Exegetical Commentary on the Epistles of St. Peter and St. Jude. International Critical Commentary.* New York: Chas. Scribner & Sons, 1905.

Broadus, John A. *Commentary on the Gospel of Matthew.* Philadelphia: American Baptist Publication Society, 1886.

Bruce, F. F. *The Epistle to the Ephesians, A Verse-by-Verse Exposition.* London: Pickering & Inglis, 1961.

———. *An Expanded Paraphrase of the Epistles of Paul,* Exeter: Paternoster, 1965.

Burrell, David James. *The Old Time Religion.* New York: American Tract Society, 1913.

Cambron, Mark G. *The New Testament, A Book-by-Book Survey.* Grand Rapids: Zondervan, 1958.

Carroll, B. H. *An Interpretation of the English Bible,* Galatians, Romans, etc. Nashville: Broadman, 1916.

———. *Sermons.* Philadelphia: American Baptist Publication Society, 1895.

Christian, John T. *A History of the Baptists.* vol. I. Nashville: Sunday School Board of the Southern Baptist Convention, 1922.

Clearwaters, Richard V. See: *The Biblical Faith of Baptists.*

Coltman, William G. *The Cathedral of Christian Truth.* Findlay, Ohio: Fundamental Truth Publishers, 1943.

Dale, R. W. *The Epistle to the Ephesians, The Expositor's Library.* London: Hodder & Stoughton, 1882.

Daniel, Carey L. *The Bible's Seeming Contradictions.* Grand Rapids: Zondervan, 1941.

Dargan, E. C. *The Doctrines of our Faith.* rev. ed. Nashville: Sunday School Board, Southern Baptist Convention, 1920.

Drew, Edward. *Studies in the Book of Romans.* Paterson, New Jersey: Madison Avenue Baptist Church, 1941.

———. *Studies in the Epistle to the Thessalonians.* Paterson, New Jersey: Madison Avenue Baptist Church, 1943.

Ellicott, Charles J. *A New Testament Commentary for English Readers.* vol. III, Ephesians & ff. by A. Barry. London: Cassell & Co., 1897.

English, E. Schuyler. *The Life and Letters of Saint Peter.* New York: Our Hope, 1941.

Evans, William. *The Great Doctrines of the Bible.* Chicago: The Bible Institute Colportage Association, 1912.

———. *Christ's Last Message to His Church, An Exposition of Revelation I–III.* New York: Revell, 1926.

Farr, Frederic W. *A Manual of Christian Doctrine.* New

York: The Alliance Press, n. d.
Ferrin, Howard W. *Strengthen Thy Brethren, A Devotional Exposition of the First Epistle of Peter.* Grand Rapids: Zondervan, 1942.
Findlay, G. G. *The Epistles to the Thessalonians, Cambridge Greek Testament.* Cambridge: University Press, 1904.
———. *The Epistle to the Ephesians, The Expositor's Bible.* 4th ed. New York: A. C. Armstrong & Son, 1899.
Foreman, Kenneth J. *God's Will and Ours.* Richmond, Va.: Outlook, 1954.
Fuller, Richard. See: Jenkens, C. A. *Baptist Doctrines.*
The Fundamentals, A Testimony to the Truth. vol. II of original 12-vol. ed. Chicago: Testimony Publishing Co., n. d.
Gaebelein, Arno C. *The Gospel of John.* 2d ed. Neptune, New Jersey, Loizeaux Brothers, 1965.
———. *The Gospel of Matthew, An Exposition.* Neptune, New Jersey, Loizeaux Brothers, 1961.
———. *Our Hope,* vol. 37, no. 11, p. 634. New York: Our Hope, May 1931.
Gladstone, W. E. *Butler's Works,* vol. I: *Analogy.* Oxford: Clarendon, 1897.
Godet, Frederick Louis. *Commentary on the Gospel of John.* vols. I–II. Grand Rapids: Zondervan, reprint from 3d ed. 1893.
———. *Commentary on St. Paul's Epistle to the Romans.* vols. I–II, Edinburgh: T. & T. Clark, 1880.
Gray, James M. *Bible Problems Explained.* 3d ed. New York: Revell, 1913.
Greene, Oliver B. *Predestination.* Greenville, South Carolina: The Gospel Hour, n. d.
Guillebaud, H. E. *Some Moral Difficulties of the Bible.* London: Inter-Varsity Fellowship, 1941.
Haldane, Robert. *Exposition of the Epistle to the Romans.* London: Banner of Truth Trust, reprint 1963.
Haldeman, I. M. *The Book of the Heavenlies, An Analysis of the Epistle to the Ephesians.* New York: Francis Emory

Fitch, Inc., n. d.

Halley, Henry H. *Pocket Bible Handbook.* Chicago: H. H. Halley, 17th ed. 1946.

Hart, J. H. A. *The First Epistle General of Peter, The Expositor's Greek Testament,* vol. V. Grand Rapids: Wm. B. Eerdmans, reprint, n. d.

Hobbs, Herschel H. *Fundamentals of our Faith.* Nashville: Broadman, 1960.

———. *What Baptists Believe.* Nashville: Broadman, 1964.

The International Standard Bible Encyclopaedia, James Orr and M. G. Kyle, editors. 5 vols. Chicago: Howard Severance Co., 1937.

Ironside, Harry A. *Full Assurance.* Chicago: Moody Press, 1937.

———. *In The Heavenlies, Addresses on Ephesians.* Neptune, New Jersey: Loizeaux Brothers, 1937.

———. *Lectures on the Book of Acts.* Neptune, New Jersey: Loizeaux Brothers, 1943.

———. *Lectures on the Epistle to the Romans.* Neptune, New Jersey: Loizeaux Brothers, 1926.

———. *What's The Answer?* Grand Rapids: Zondervan, 1944.

Jacobs, Henry E. *A Summary of the Christian Faith.* Philadelphia: United Lutheran Publishing House, 1905.

Jamieson, Robert, A. R. Fausset, and David Brown. *A Commentary, Critical and Explanatory, on the Old and New Testaments.* Hartford, Connecticut: S. S. Scranton, 1871.

Jenkens, Charles A., editor. *Baptist Doctrines.* St. Louis, Missouri: Chancy R. Barnes, 1882.

Jeter, Jeremiah B. *Baptist Principles Reset.* 3rd ed. Richmond, Virginia: The Religious Herald Co., 1902.

Johnson, E. H., and Henry G. Weston. *An Outline of Systematic Theology.* 2d ed. Philadelphia: American Baptist Publication Society, 1895.

Keyser, Leander S. *Election and Conversion.* Burlington, Iowa: Lutheran Literary Board, 1914.

Knowling, R. J. *The Acts of the Apostles, The Expositor's*

Greek Testament. New York: Dodd, Mead & Co., 1900.

Lightfoot, Joseph B. *Notes on the Epistles of St. Paul.* Grand Rapids: Zondervan, reprint 1957.

———. *St. Paul's Epistle to the Philippians.* Grand Rapids: Zondervan, reprint 1956.

Lightner, Robert. *Doctrine of God* (Adult Student Quarterly). Des Plaines, Illinois: Regular Baptist Press, 1967.

Lockyer, Herbert. *All The Doctrines of the Bible.* Grand Rapids: Zondervan, 1964.

Lorimer, George C. *Charles Haddon Spurgeon.* Boston: James H. Earle, 1892.

Lumby, J. Rawson. *The Acts of the Apostles, The Cambridge Bible for Schools and Colleges.* Cambridge: University Press, 1884.

Luther, Martin. *Commentary on the Epistle to the Romans,* translated by J. Theodore Mueller. Grand Rapids: Zondervan, 1954.

Maclaren, Alexander. *Expositions of Holy Scripture.* 25 vols. New York: Hodder & Stoughton and George H. Doran Co., n. d.

Mantey, Julius R. *See:* Turner, George A.

McQuilkin, Robert C. *The Message of Romans, An Exposition.* Grand Rapids: Zondervan, 1947.

Meyer, F. B. *Christian Living.* Philadelphia: Henry Altemus Co., n. d.

———. *Through the Bible Day by Day.* Philadelphia: American Sunday School Union, 1914.

———. *Tried By Fire, Expositions of the First Epistle of Peter.* London: Marshall, Morgan & Scott, 1950.

———. *The Way Into the Holiest, Expositions of Hebrews.* New York: Revell, 1893.

Milligan, William and William F. Moulton. *The Gospel According to John, The International Revision Commentary on the New Testament,* ed. by Philip Schaff. New York: Chas. Scribner's Sons, 1883.

Moody, D. L. *Select Sermons.* Chicago: Moody Press, 1881.

Morgan, G. Campbell. *The Acts of the Apostles.* New York:

Revell, 1924.
———. *The Analyzed Bible,* Introduction, Matthew to Revelation. New York: Revell, 1908.
———. *God's Methods With Men.* New York: Revell, 1898.
———. *The Gospel According to John.* New York: Revell, n. d.
———. *The Gospel According to Matthew.* 5th ed. New York: Revell, 1929.
———. *Living Messages of the Books of The Bible, Matthew To Colossians.* New York: Revell, 1912.
———. *The Westminster Pulpit.* vols. I–X. New York: Revell, 1954.
Moule, H. C. G. *The Second Epistle to Timothy, A Devotional Commentary.* 4th impression. London: The Religious Tract Society, 1906.
———. *The Epistle to the Romans, The Cambridge Bible for Schools.* Cambridge: University Press, 1881.
Moulton, William F. See: Milligan, William.
Mullins, Edgar Y. *Baptist Beliefs.* 4th ed. Philadelphia: Judson, 1925.
———. *The Christian Religion in its Doctrinal Expression.* Nashville: Broadman, 1917. 12th reprint.
Neighbour, R. E. *The Baptism in the Holy Ghost, or Before and After Pentecost: An Exegesis of Acts 1 and 2.* Cleveland, Ohio: Union Gospel Press, 1930.
Orr, James. *Sidelights on Christian Doctrine.* New York: A. C. Armstrong & Son, 1909.
———. *See also: International Standard Bible Encyclopaedia.*
Pardington, George P. *Outline Studies in Christian Doctrine.* New York: Christian Alliance, 1916.
Pendleton, J. M. *Christian Doctrines.* Philadelphia: American Baptist Publication Society, 1878.
Pettingill, William L. *Bible Questions Answered.* 3d ed. Wilmington, Delaware: Just A Word Inc., 1935.
———. *Simple Studies in Matthew.* 5th ed. Philadelphia: Philadelphia School of the Bible, 1910.

Pierson, Arthur T. *The Believer's Life: Its Past, Present, and Future Tenses.* London: Morgan and Scott, 1905.

———. *Seed Thoughts For Public Speakers,* New York: Funk and Wagnalls, 1916.

Pieters, Albertus. *The Facts and Mysteries of the Christian Faith.* 3d ed. Grand Rapids: Wm. B. Eerdmans, 1939.

Plummer, Alfred. *The Gospel According to St. John, The Cambridge Bible for Schools and Colleges.* Cambridge: University Press, 1912.

The Pulpit Commentary, edited by Spence & Exell. New York: Funk & Wagnalls, n. d.

Rackham, Richard B. *The Acts of the Apostles, An Exposition.* 14th ed. reprint 1953. London: Methuen & Co., 1901.

Reith, George. *The Gospel According to St. John.* vols. I–II. Edinburgh: T. & T. Clark, 1889. 8th reprint, 1959.

Rice, N. L. *God Sovereign and Man Free.* Philadelphia: Presbyterian Board of Publication, 1850.

Riley, William B. *The Bible of the Expositor and the Evangelist.* 40 vols. Cleveland, Ohio: Union Gospel Press, 1926 and ff.

Robertson, Archibald T. *Commentary on the Gospel According to Matthew* (The Bible for Home and School). New York: Macmillan, 1911.

———. *Word Pictures in the New Testament.* vols. I–VI. New York: Harper & Bros., 1930.

Rowley, H. H. *The Biblical Doctrine of Election.* London: Lutterworth, 2d impression, 1952.

Ryle, J. C. *Expository Thoughts on the Gospels, St. John.* vol. II. 6th ed. London: Wm. Hunt & Co., 1883.

Sanday, William, and Arthur C. Headlam. *A Critical and Exegetical Commentary on the Epistle to the Romans.* 4th ed. *International Critical Commentary* series. Edinburgh: T. & T. Clark, 1900.

Scofield, C. I. *In Many Pulpits With C. I. Scofield.* Grand Rapids: Baker Book House, 1966, reprint.

———. *Scofield Bible Correspondence Course.* vols. II, III.

Chicago: Moody Bible Institute, 1907.
Scroggie, W. Graham. *The Unfolding Drama of Redemption.* vol. II. London: Pickering & Inglis, 1957.
Smith, Justin A. *Commentary on the Epistle to the Ephesians,* in *An American Commentary on the New Testament, Corinthians to Thessalonians.* Philadelphia: American Baptist Publication Society, 1891.
Spurgeon, Charles H. *All of Grace.* London: Passmore and Alabaster, 1887.
———. *The Autobiography of Charles H. Spurgeon.* vols. I–IV. Philadelphia: American Baptist Publication Society, n. d.
———. *The Best Bread, Sermons Preached in 1887.* New York and London: Funk & Wagnalls, 1891.
———. *Commenting and Commentaries.* Grand Rapids: Kregel Publications, reprint 1954.
———. *Feathers for Arrows.* London: Passmore and Alabaster, 1870.
———. *Illustrations and Meditations, or Flowers from a Puritan's Garden.* New York: Funk & Wagnalls, 1883.
———. *Sermons: Memorial Library.* vol. V. New York: Funk & Wagnalls, 1859.
———. *Spurgeon's Lectures to his Students,* ed. by David Otis Fuller, 3d ed. Grand Rapids: Zondervan, 1945.
———. *The Treasury of the New Testament.* vols. I–IV. Grand Rapids: Zondervan, reprint, 1950.
Stifler, James M. *An Introduction to the Acts of the Apostles.* New York: Revell, 1892.
———. *The Epistle to the Romans.* New York: Revell, 1897.
Stokes, G. T. *The Acts of the Apostles. The Expositor's Bible.* vols. I–II. London: Hodder & Stoughton, 1891.
Strauss, Lehman. *The Atonement of Christ.* Findlay, Ohio: Dunham Publ. Co., 1959.
———. *The Book of the Revelation.* Neptune, New Jersey: Loizeaux Brothers, 1964.
Strong, Augustus H. *Systematic Theology.* Philadelphia: Judson, 1907.

Thiessen, Henry C. *Introductory Lectures in Systematic Theology*. Grand Rapids: Wm. B. Eerdmans, 1949.

Thomas, W. H. Griffith. *The Principles of Theology*. London: Longmans, Green & Co., 1930.

———. *St. Paul's Epistle to the Romans, A Devotional Commentary*. vols. I–III. London: The Religious Tract Society, 1911.

Torrey, Reuben A. *The Importance and Value of Proper Bible Study*. Chicago: Moody Press, 1921.

———. *Practical and Perplexing Questions Answered*. New York: Revell, 1898.

———. *What the Bible Teaches*. New York: Revell, 1898.

Trench, Richard C. *Epistles to the Seven Churches of Asia*. New York: Chas. Scribner's Sons, 1862.

Truett, George W. *The Prophet's Mantle*. Grand Rapids: Wm. B. Eerdmans, 1948.

———. *A Quest for Souls*. New York: Doubleday, Doran & Co., 1929.

Trumbull, H. Clay. *How to Deal with Doubts and Doubters*. rev. ed. London: Marshall Bros., 1907.

Tuck, Robert. *A Handbook of Biblical Difficulties*. 2d series. New York: Thomas Whittaker, 1890.

Turner, George A., and Julius R. Mantey. *The Gospel According to John, The Evangelical Commentary*. Grand Rapids: Wm. B. Eerdmans, 1964.

Underwood, A. C. *A History of the English Baptists*, London: The Baptist Union of Great Britain and Ireland, 1947.

Vedder, Henry C. *A Short History of the Baptists*. new ed. Philadelphia: American Baptist Publication Society, 1907.

Vincent, Marvin R. *Word Studies in the New Testament*. vols. I–IV. New York: Chas. Scribner's Sons, 1924.

Vine, W. E. *An Expository Dictionary of New Testament Words*. vols. I–IV. London: Oliphants Ltd., 1940.

Wall, A. J. *The Truth About Election*. Texarkana, Arkansas-Texas: The Baptist Sunday School Committee, n. d.

Wallace, O. C. S. *What Baptists Believe: The New Hampshire Confession, An Exposition.* Nashville: Sunday School Board of the Southern Baptist Convention, 1913.

Weiss, Bernhard. *The Religion of the New Testament.* New York: Funk & Wagnalls, 1905.

White, W. R. *Baptist Distinctives.* Nashville: Sunday School Board, Southern Baptist Convention, 1946.

Wood, Nathan E. *The Person and Work of Jesus Christ, An Exposition of Christian Doctrine.* Philadelphia: American Baptist Publication Society, 1908.

Wordsworth, Christopher. *The New Testament in the Original Greek, with Notes and Introductions.* London, Oxford, and Cambridge: Rivingtons, 1877.

ACKNOWLEDGMENTS

Appreciation is expressed to the following publishers for permission to quote from material in works of authors of which they hold the copyright, as further indicated where the citation appears and/or in the bibliography:

American Baptist Board of Education and Publication, Valley Forge, Pennsylvania

E. Y. Mullins: *The Christian Religion In Its Doctrinal Expression*

American Sunday-School Union, Philadelphia, Pennsylvania

F. B. Meyer: *Through The Bible Day by Day,* vol. VI

Baker Book House, Grand Rapids, Michigan

C. I. Scofield: *In Many Pulpits*

Wm. B. Eerdmans Publishing Co., Grand Rapids, Michigan

H. C. G. Moule: in *International Standard Bible Encyclopaedia*

Albertus Pieters: *Facts and Mysteries of the Christian Faith*

H. C. Thiessen: *Lectures in Systematic Theology*

George W. Truett: *A Quest For Souls*

G. A. Turner and J. R. Mantey: *The Gospel According to John*

Moody Press, Chicago, Illinois

W. E. Biederwolf: *Later Evangelistic Sermons*

H. A. Ironside: *Full Assurance*

R. A. Torrey: *The Importance and Value of Proper Bible Study*

Outlook Publishers, Richmond, Virginia
K. J. Foreman: *God's Will And Ours*
Pickering & Inglis, Ltd.
F. F. Bruce: *Epistle to the Ephesians*
Fleming H. Revell Company, Old Tappan, New Jersey
William Evans: *Christ's Last Message To His Church*
G. C. Morgan: *Acts of The Apostles; The Gospel According To Matthew; Westminster Pulpit,* vol. VII
The Sunday School Board of the Southern Baptist Convention, Nashville, Tennessee
B. H. Carroll, *An Interpretation of the English Bible*
J. T. Christian, *A History of the Baptists,* vol. I
E. C. Dargan, *The Doctrines of Our Faith,* revised edition
H. H. Hobbs, *What Baptists Believe; Fundamentals of Our Faith*
A. T. Robertson, *Word Pictures in the New Testament,* vols. III, IV, VI
W. R. White, *Baptist Distinctives*
Union Gospel Press, Cleveland, Ohio
R. E. Neighbour: *The Baptism of the Holy Ghost*
W. B. Riley: *The Bible of the Expositor and the Evangelist,* vols. 9,12
Zondervan Publishing House, Grand Rapids, Michigan
M. G. Cambron: *The New Testament, A Book-by-Book Survey*
W. G. Coltman: *The Cathedral of Christian Truth* (Dunham)
C. L. Daniel: *The Bible's Seeming Contradictions*
H. W. Ferrin: *Strengthen Thy Brethren*
H. H. Halley: *Pocket Bible Handbook*
H. A. Ironside: *What's The Answer?*
Herbert Lockyer: *All The Doctrines of The Bible*
Martin Luther: *Commentary on The Epistle to The Romans*
R. C. McQuilkin: *The Message of Romans*
Lehman Strauss: *The Atonement of Christ* (Dunham)

INDEX TO SCRIPTURE REFERENCES

INDEX TO NAMES

The fact that Christ died for all men, makes me interested in the salvation of all men.

Elisabeth Elliot (widow of missionary Jim Elliot, who was martyred in 1956, while attempting to reach the Auca Indians of Ecuador with the gospel for the very first time).

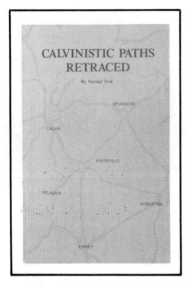